AVOID BUSINESS KILLER

Shielding Your Business From Fatal Mistakes

By

Michael Werki

COPYRIGHT NOTICE

TABLE OF CONTENTS

INTRODUCTION

In today's fast-paced and ever-changing business environment, entrepreneurs and leaders are continually presented with multiple problems that may make or ruin their operations. From tough rivalry and economic downturns to weak leadership and lack of innovation, innumerable elements might convert a growing organization into a mere memory. In this book, "**Avoid Business Killer**," we go into evaluating the numerous traps and errors that entrepreneurs typically make and present practical suggestions on how to prevent them.

Every entrepreneur commences on their company journey with the finest intentions, equipped with creative ideas and a burning drive for success. However, as the phrase goes, "**The path to success is paved with failures.**" It is crucial to identify and learn from these errors to avoid them from becoming company killers.

Through thorough research, case studies, and personal experiences, this book attempts to equip entrepreneurs with informed guidance on how to navigate the hazardous seas of the business world.

We investigate numerous areas that pose challenges to a company's lifespan, such as insufficient financial management, poor marketing tactics, inadequate market research, and a lack of flexibility.

The first chapter of this book digs into the necessity of having a solid foundation for every organization - financial management. We will address the main financial errors that entrepreneurs make, such as underestimating expenses, mismanaging cash flow, and forgetting to construct a rainy-day reserve. Readers will discover practical advice on budgeting, managing debt, and building financial controls to prevent the mistakes that may lead to financial ruin.

In the next chapters, we will study the vital function of marketing in guaranteeing corporate success. Entrepreneurs frequently fall into the trap of seeing marketing as an afterthought or a luxury they cannot afford. However, efficient marketing is not only crucial for acquiring and maintaining consumers but also for developing a strong brand presence in the market. By studying issues such as target market identification, branding, digital marketing tactics, and customer relationship management, we educate entrepreneurs with practical guidance on how to avoid typical marketing blunders and develop a good marketing strategy.

The book also dives into the pitfalls of disregarding market research and failing to adapt to the shifting business scene. We analyze case studies of organizations that failed owing to their failure to anticipate market trends and accept new technology. We present a step-by-step tutorial on how to do market research successfully and underline the necessity of being ahead of the curve in terms of innovation and adjusting to market needs.

Throughout the book, we highlight the necessity of strong leadership and good decision-making. We emphasize the implications of bad leadership and the influence it may have on a business's performance. We share insights on leadership types and methods that may help entrepreneurs avoid typical leadership blunders and motivate their teams to achieve greatness.

In conclusion, "**Avoid Business Killer**" provides a thorough reference for entrepreneurs and company executives who seek to stay clear of the hazards and blunders that might lead to the destruction of their companies. By concentrating on financial management, marketing tactics, market research, adaptation, and leadership, this book gives readers the skills and information they need to develop a resilient and successful organization. Whether you are a seasoned entrepreneur or just starting, this book will serve as a vital resource to assist you avoid the business killers that might obstruct your road to success.

CHAPTER 1:

UNDERSTANDING BUSINESS KILLERS

Avoiding business killers is vital for the success and survival of any firm. These are elements that may greatly impair a company's development and even lead to its demise if not handled in a timely way. Understanding and being proactive in avoiding business killers is vital for entrepreneurs and company owners.

One of the biggest business killers is inadequate financial management. Many firms fail owing to insufficient cash flow management, inappropriate budgeting, and lack of financial planning. Neglecting these issues may lead to mounting debts, inability to pay suppliers and workers, and finally, bankruptcy. Entrepreneurs must build a sound financial strategy, analyze their spending, and frequently check their financial accounts to discover any possible concerns early on.

Another business killer is inadequate marketing and targeting. A lack of awareness of your target market, failure to find the correct marketing channels, or not responding to changing client wants may significantly harm a business's success. It is vital to devote time and money to market research, recognizing consumer preferences, and executing efficient marketing tactics to attract and keep clients.

Failure to adapt to technology and shifting trends is also a typical business killer. In today's fast-paced world, technology plays a key role in practically every element of corporate operations. Failing to accept new technology, simplify procedures, and remain informed about industry developments may lead to inefficiencies, lost production, and being left behind by rivals.

To prevent this, companies should invest in modernizing their systems, educating their personnel, and keeping a close watch on developing trends that may affect their sector.

Additionally, bad leadership and management may be damaging to a business's growth.

Ineffective decision-making, lack of communication, micromanagement, and a toxic work culture may lead to discontent among workers, high turnover rates, and lower productivity. Business owners should concentrate on enhancing their leadership and management abilities, maintaining an open and friendly work atmosphere, and offering clear instructions and expectations for their staff.

Lastly, a lack of innovation and an inability to adapt to a changing market may be a company killer. The business environment is continuously altering, and organizations that fail to innovate and stay up with increasing customer needs risk becoming outdated. It is vital for entrepreneurs to invest in research and development, foster innovation and out-of-the-box thinking within their teams, and regularly analyze their goods and services to remain relevant and competitive.

Conclusion, identifying and avoiding business killers is crucial for the long-term success of any firm. By proactively addressing challenges such as poor financial management, inefficient marketing, opposition to technology and change, ineffective leadership, and lack of innovation, enterprise owners may guarantee that their firm not only survives but flourishes in a competitive environment. By keeping proactive, consistently learning and adapting, and having a strong sense of awareness about possible business killers, entrepreneurs may navigate through hurdles and develop a firm basis for their company's success.

DEFINITION AND EXPLANATION OF BUSINESS KILLERS

Business killers refer to external forces or internal blunders that can seriously damage or even bring down a corporation. They may be unplanned incidents or blunders that can interrupt the usual working of a firm, resulting in large financial losses, harm to reputation, loss of clients, and occasionally even bankruptcy. To ensure the life and profitability of a firm, it is vital to detect and prevent these business killers.

One typical company killer is inadequate financial management or lack of financial control. This happens when a firm fails to successfully manage its cash flow, planning, or accounting systems. Without expert financial planning and analysis, a firm might rapidly find itself in a perilous financial situation. This might lead to an inability to pay payments, defaulting on debts, and the final collapse of the firm.

Another key business killer is neglecting consumer requirements and feedback. In today's extremely competitive economy, client happiness is crucial. Failing to listen to consumers, adapt to their changing expectations, or disregarding negative feedback may swiftly lead to a fall in sales and a loss of client loyalty. Additionally, with the introduction of social media, angry consumers may quickly share their unpleasant experiences, harming a company's brand dramatically. It is crucial to emphasize customer satisfaction, react to feedback immediately, and take proactive actions to remedy any problems or concerns made by consumers.

A company killer that is frequently neglected is inadequate personnel management or a poisonous work environment. Employees are the backbone of every successful firm, and their morale, productivity, and contentment play a critical part in the overall success of the organization. Neglecting to invest in sufficient training, neglecting to give development opportunities, or not resolving disagreements and concerns within the workplace may result in high turnover rates, lower productivity, and a poor business culture. Company owners and managers must establish a healthy work atmosphere, develop open communication, and ensure that workers feel appreciated and supported.

Ineffective marketing and branding initiatives may also be damaging to a firm. In today's digital world, when customers are continuously overwhelmed with information and alternatives, differentiating from the competition is crucial. Failing to build a strong and distinctive brand identity, not investing in effective marketing initiatives, or not adjusting to shifting marketing trends may lead to a loss of market share and lower revenues. Companies need to remain up-to-date with marketing methods and adopt creative ways to reach and interact with their target audience.

Lastly, disregarding or failing to adapt to technological improvements may be a company killer in today's fast-paced and technology-driven environment. Technology plays a key part in contemporary corporate operations, and organizations that fail to exploit technology efficiently may rapidly be left behind. This might include antiquated systems, inefficient operations, or a lack of digital presence. Embracing technology innovations may simplify corporate processes, boost efficiency, enhance client experiences, and give a competitive advantage.

To prevent these business killers, organizations need to prioritize risk management, maintain solid financial monitoring, aggressively listen to and handle consumer feedback, engage in personnel training and development, build successful marketing strategies, and embrace technology. Regularly monitoring and analyzing potential business killers, and taking proactive efforts to limit risks, may help firms overcome hurdles and maintain their long-term prosperity.

By keeping watchful and adaptive in an ever-changing business world, firms may avoid becoming victims of business killers and assure their continuous development and profitability.

IMPORTANCE OF IDENTIFYING AND AVOIDING BUSINESS KILLERS

Identifying and avoiding business killers is of the highest significance for every entrepreneur or company owner. A business killer refers to any element or scenario that might adversely affect the success and sustainability of a firm. These killers might vary from internal concerns like bad management choices or inadequate tactics to external reasons like economic downturns or changing market dynamics.

One fundamental reason why it is crucial to recognize and prevent business killers is that they may lead to considerable financial losses. For example, bad financial management methods, such as inappropriate budgeting or overextending credit, may swiftly deplete a company's resources and even lead to bankruptcy. By being proactive and detecting the signals of possible company killers, entrepreneurs can take preemptive actions to avoid financial risks and assure long-term stability.

Furthermore, avoiding business killers is vital for keeping a great brand image. Oftentimes, business killers emerge from reputation-damaging situations, such as product recalls, ethical scandals, or public relations catastrophes. These unfavorable incidents may ruin a company's image, undermine consumer trust, and result in a loss of market share. By recognizing the possible challenges that might hurt the brand and taking action to prevent them, companies can safeguard their reputation and sustain client loyalty.

Moreover, by avoiding business killers, entrepreneurs may secure the sustainability and development of their firms. For example, neglecting to adapt to shifting market trends or technical improvements may swiftly leave a corporation old and useless. By detecting these potential business killers, entrepreneurs can build strategies and invest in resources that enable them to remain competitive and satisfy the shifting demands of their target market. This proactive strategy may help organizations to survive in dynamic and competitive sectors.

Identifying and avoiding business killers also cultivates a culture of constant development and innovation inside a firm. By routinely analyzing the business environment and recognizing possible challenges, firms may promote proactive thinking and problem-solving among their staff. This approach offers possibilities for innovation and builds a culture of adaptation, helping firms to remain ahead of the curve and grab new development opportunities.

In all, detecting and avoiding business killers is of the highest significance for entrepreneurs and company owners. By doing so, organizations may defend their financial stability, maintain a strong brand image, sustain growth, and develop a culture of innovation. It takes a proactive and watchful attitude to detect possible hazards and take the required procedures to neutralize them. Ultimately, by avoiding business killers, entrepreneurs position their firms for long-term success and resilience in an ever-changing and competitive market.

COMMON TYPES OF BUSINESS KILLERS

In today's extremely competitive and dynamic business world, one key factor that every entrepreneur and company owner must concentrate on is avoiding the frequent sorts of business killers. These are elements that may greatly affect the success and longevity of a firm, ultimately leading to its demise. By proactively recognizing and addressing these variables, firms may boost their chances of survival and assure long-term success.

1. Poor financial management: Inadequate financial management is one of the biggest company killers. Without adequate financial planning, budgeting, and effective cash flow management, companies may soon find themselves in a perilous situation. It is necessary to build solid financial systems and routinely analyze financial performance to reduce the hazards associated with inadequate financial management.

2. Lack of market research and comprehension: Not completely knowing the target market and neglecting to undertake market research may be a

deadly error for any organization. Without a strong grasp of consumers' requirements, tastes, and buying behavior, it becomes impossible to produce products or services that connect with the market. Investing in market research and regularly monitoring industry developments may help a firm remain ahead of the competition.

3. Inability to adapt to change: In today's fast-paced corporate scene, flexibility is vital to survival. Businesses that are reluctant to change or fail to innovate risk becoming obsolete. Whether it's keeping up with technology improvements, shifts in customer tastes, or changes in the competitive environment, a lack of adaptability may be disastrous to a firm. Firms need to be adaptable, accept new ideas, and be prepared to pivot their strategy as required.

4. Poor leadership and management: Effective leadership and management are crucial for the success of any firm. Incompetent or incompetent leaders may create a hostile work climate, inhibit cooperation, and make bad strategic judgments. It is vital to invest in leadership development and

establish a healthy business culture that empowers people and fosters productivity and creativity.

5. Lack of customer focus: Customers are the lifeblood of every firm, and neglecting to prioritize their requirements may lead to failure. Businesses that do not place enough focus on customer happiness, service quality, and creating strong customer connections risk losing their client base to competition. Regular contact with consumers, receiving feedback, and making required modifications are vital for sustaining a customer-centric strategy.

6. Failure to adapt to technology: Technology plays a key part in the development and growth of contemporary organizations. Companies that do not exploit technology properly or fail to keep up with digital innovations risk falling behind. Whether it's developing a good web presence, adopting automation technologies, or leveraging data analytics to drive business choices, embracing technology is vital for remaining competitive in today's digital world.

7. Insufficient marketing and branding: Businesses that disregard the significance of marketing and branding frequently struggle to attract consumers and develop a strong brand presence. Effective marketing techniques, including online and offline advertising, social media interaction, and brand storytelling, are vital for reaching target audiences and building brand recognition.

To prevent these typical sorts of company killers, entrepreneurs, and business owners must focus on constant learning, adaptation, and being informed about market developments. Regularly monitoring and managing risks, engaging in strategic planning, and harnessing technology for company development may considerably boost the odds of long-term success. By being proactive in reducing these possible dangers, organizations may position themselves for development, profitability, and sustainability.

IMPACT OF BUSINESS KILLERS ON ORGANIZATIONS

In this setting, understanding the effect of these business killers on businesses becomes crucial.

One prominent consequence of business killers is the deterioration in financial performance. When businesses fail to address and mitigate business killers, they may suffer from serious financial losses. For example, bad financial management, insufficient cost control measures, or inefficient marketing techniques may lead to fewer sales, higher expenditures, and eventually, reduced profitability. This negative financial effect might hamper an organization's capacity to invest in future initiatives, attract investors, or get critical finance for development and expansion.

Moreover, business killers may also have a bad influence on staff morale, engagement, and retention. Employees are the backbone of every corporation, and when they feel the effects of business killers, it may result in higher stress levels, job discontent, and diminished motivation. For instance, bad leadership, insufficient training and development programs, or an uncomfortable work environment may dramatically impair employee productivity and dedication, eventually leading to a greater employee turnover rate. This may further burden the firm with recruiting and training expenditures, not to mention the possible loss of valued personnel.

Additionally, the reputation and brand image of a corporation may be adversely harmed by business killers. In today's digital era, news travels swiftly, and unfavorable tales or experiences may ruin a company's brand almost instantaneously. For example, a product recall owing to safety concerns, a publicized staff misbehavior episode, or a breach of consumer data may all have a lasting influence on how the public sees the firm. This might result in decreasing consumer trust, loss of clients, and difficulties in acquiring new customers. Rebuilding a tainted image may be a laborious and expensive process that may take years, if not decades, to completely recover.

Furthermore, business killers may hamper innovation and impair the organization's capacity to respond to market developments. In today's quickly developing business world, firms must be nimble and responsive to new technology, consumer expectations, and competitive threats. However, if a company is consumed with internal challenges created by business killers, it may struggle to deploy resources and concentrate on innovation and adaptability. This might result in lost opportunities, outmoded goods or services, and the inability to keep ahead of the market.

Additionally, it is necessary to continually review and evaluate possible business killers that may occur in the future. By keeping proactive and watchful, companies may recognize and handle these concerns before they become serious difficulties. This entails completing rigorous risk assessments, adopting strong internal controls, and developing a culture of continuous improvement.

Organizations should also promote excellent communication and openness. By ensuring that all stakeholders are informed and involved, potential business killers may be detected and handled in a timely way. This involves conveying objectives, plans, and performance expectations to staff, as well as routinely requesting feedback and input from customers and suppliers. By encouraging open and honest communication channels, businesses may proactively detect and prevent potential business killers.

Ultimately, preventing business killers demands a proactive and comprehensive strategy. It requires a mix of risk management, effective leadership, workforce involvement, and strategic decision-making. By being sensitive to possible dangers and implementing preventive steps, businesses may enhance their resilience and position themselves for long-term success. In doing so, they may limit the negative effects of business killers and instead concentrate on achieving development, profitability, and good organizational results.

In conclusion, the effect of business killers on companies is enormous and may have far-reaching implications. By avoiding these business killers via strategic planning, good management practices, and a focus on continuous improvement, firms can maintain their financial performance, employee morale, reputation, and capacity to innovate. Prioritizing risk management, open communication, and proactive decision-making are critical measures in avoiding business killers and assuring the long-term survival of the firm.

CHAPTER 2: POOR FINANCIAL MANAGEMENT

Poor financial management may be disastrous to any organization since it can lead to huge losses and even result in the collapse of the firm. Hence, firms need to prevent this business killer by establishing efficient strategies and exercising strong financial management.

One of the key reasons why bad financial Management is a company killer is the absence of precise financial records and recordkeeping. Without effective record-keeping, it becomes hard for companies to manage their revenue, spending, and overall financial health. This might result in cash flow concerns, as organizations may struggle to pay invoices or handle payments on time. Additionally, it becomes tough to understand financial patterns and make educated choices without precise financial data.

Another component of bad financial management is not taking the time to prepare a precise budget and forecast for the organization. A budget acts as a blueprint, helping organizations to plan and allocate resources efficiently. Without a budget, firms may overspend, compromising financial stability and the capacity to engage in development possibilities. Lack of forecasting may also contribute to poor decision-making, as organizations may not foresee market shifts, resulting in lost opportunities or excessive risk-taking.

Furthermore, bad financial management involves the inability to develop and maintain sound financial controls. These controls are important to avoid fraud, maintain compliance with legislation, and secure firm assets. When organizations lack to create effective financial controls, they put themselves up to a variety of hazards. This may involve embezzlement, false financial reporting, and unlawful usage of corporate cash.

Moreover, weak financial controls may threaten the confidence of investors, lenders, and other stakeholders, leading to a loss of reputation and significant legal ramifications.

In addition to these dangers, bad financial management typically implies overlooking the necessity of cash flow management. Without diligent monitoring and preparation, companies might find themselves suffering cash shortages and unable to satisfy their financial responsibilities. This might result in delayed payments to suppliers, lost chances for expansion, and even bankruptcy.

Another significant feature of bad financial management is the inability to effectively manage debt and leverage. Taking on too much debt without a clear repayment plan may dramatically strain a business's financial health and creditworthiness. High-interest payments, late fees, and penalties may chew up corporate resources and limit development.

Finally, bad financial management may express itself via an insufficient grasp of financial ratios and key performance indicators (KPIs). These are crucial instruments that give insights into a business's financial status and performance. Ignoring or misinterpreting these cues may lead to faulty decision-making and ultimately, financial instability.

To avoid the business killer of bad financial management, businesses must emphasize financial literacy and ensure they have staff with the appropriate skills and knowledge in financial management. This involves employing specialists such as accountants or financial consultants who may give assistance and help. It is also vital for firms to invest in comprehensive accounting software and systems that allow precise record-keeping, budgeting, and forecasting.

A vital step in preventing bad money management is setting a precise budget and constantly reviewing and revising it as circumstances change. This will assist firms keep on track with their spending, revenue objectives, and cash flow management. Additionally, firms should implement and maintain solid financial controls to avoid fraud and assure compliance.

Proactive cash flow management is crucial, and organizations should monitor their inflows and outflows constantly. This involves routinely assessing payment terms with customers, negotiating advantageous terms with suppliers, and managing working capital properly.

Furthermore, companies must manage their debt responsibly, by carefully analyzing the need for borrowing, formulating a repayment plan, and investigating ways to refinance or consolidate debt when required. Monitoring financial ratios and KPIs and frequently benchmarking against industry standards may also give significant insights and assist identify areas that need development.

Overall, bad financial management may be a company killer, but with an emphasis on accurate record-keeping, budgeting, good financial controls, cash flow management, debt management, and financial literacy, firms can limit the risks and assure long-term financial stability and success. By taking proactive actions to prevent this business killer, firms may position themselves for sustained development and profitability.

In conclusion, bad financial management may be a devastating business killer that can lead to large losses and possibly the bankruptcy of a firm. Firms must emphasize precise record-keeping, construct a clear budget and forecast, implement solid financial controls, and aggressively monitor cash flow, debt, and financial ratios. By doing so, firms may avoid the dangers of bad financial management and pave the road to long-term success.

LACK OF BUDGETING AND FINANCIAL PLANNING

Setting up and sustaining a successful company is a tough venture that demands careful preparation and execution. One essential factor that may frequently make or ruin a corporation is the absence of budgeting and financial planning. This inability to efficiently handle funds may be devastating to both existing organizations and startups alike, leading to substantial ramifications and even the collapse of the company.

First and foremost, a lack of budgeting and financial planning means operating without a clear blueprint for financial success. Without a well-structured budget in place, firms are more likely to overpay, underspend in important areas, or distribute resources inefficiently. This lack of management may result in increased expenses, decreased cash flow, and an inability to satisfy financial responsibilities, such as paying suppliers or staff. It may also restrict the capacity to engage in projects that would promote development and prevent the organization from capitalizing on prospective commercial prospects.

Furthermore, without good financial planning, firms may quickly enter into a cycle of amassing debt. This not only puts an extra burden on cash flow but also exposes the organization to probable insolvency or bankruptcy. Insufficient finances to sustain ongoing operations, repay debts, or manage unanticipated financial losses may swiftly kill a firm, as financial institutions grow unwilling to grant more financing or assistance. Consequently, the absence of budgeting and financial planning may trap firms in a downward cycle, making it exceedingly tough to recover and achieve financial stability.

Moreover, insufficient financial preparation might lead to poor decision-making. Without a comprehensive grasp of the company's present financial status and future predictions, business leaders may make misinformed decisions that adversely harm the organization. This might involve signing into unprofitable contracts or partnerships, overinvesting in non-essential sectors, or disregarding vital investments required for development and sustainability.

Additionally, a lack of financial planning might hamper a business's capacity to adapt and react to market developments. By not examining market trends, consumer behavior, and competitor activities, organizations lose out on crucial information that may guide strategic choices. Without examining these aspects, organizations may fail to manage resources efficiently, overlook possible income opportunities, or fall behind their competitors.

To prevent the company killer which is the absence of budgeting and financial planning, organizations must emphasize these key factors. Implementing budgeting procedures and frequently analyzing financial performance, estimating income and spending, and establishing targets are key tasks. Seeking expert counsel from accountants or financial consultants may also give useful insight and help. Developing a detailed financial strategy that matches the company's strategic goals and periodically evaluating and revising it as required is vital for success and long-term sustainability.

In conclusion, weak budgeting and financial planning pose major dangers to firms of all sizes. The lack of control over money, the buildup of debt, poor decision-making, and an inability to react to market changes may all contribute to a business's failure. Company owners must emphasize budgeting and financial planning to maintain financial stability, make educated choices, and optimize development potential. By doing so, firms may avoid becoming victims of this business killer and develop a strong basis for long-term success.

INADEQUATE CASH FLOW MANAGEMENT

Cash flow is the lifeblood of a firm. It is the flow of money in and out of a firm, and it is vital for the smooth running and development of any corporation. Inadequate cash flow management is a big difficulty that many organizations confront, and if left ignored, it may become a company killer. Therefore, understanding and properly managing cash flow is vital to guarantee the long-term survival of any organization.

One of the primary reasons insufficient cash flow management may be damaging to a firm is the failure to satisfy financial commitments quickly. When a firm does not have enough cash on hand to pay its suppliers, workers, or creditors on time, it may lead to broken relationships and loss of reputation. Furthermore, missed payments may result in extra charges like late fees or penalties, harming the company's profitability and overall financial health.

Another consequence of inadequate cash flow management is the inability to invest in growth prospects or handle unanticipated costs. Without appropriate capital reserves, firms lose out on chances to grow, buy new assets, or engage in research and development.

Additionally, unforeseen occurrences like equipment failures, legal challenges, or natural catastrophes might strike at any moment, necessitating emergency monetary outlays. If a firm is not prepared to absorb these unforeseen expenditures, it may be compelled to suspend operations or take on costly loans, further stressing its financial situation.

Furthermore, insufficient cash flow management might lead to issues in paying wages and benefits to workers. This may result in poorer staff morale, decreased productivity, and probable attrition. Employees depend on their paychecks to satisfy their financial commitments, and if a firm frequently fails to pay them on time, it may create a hostile work atmosphere and undermine the company's image as an employer of choice.

To prevent these potential business killers, organizations need to develop efficient cash flow management methods. This begins with proper forecasting and budgeting to predict future financial inputs and expenditures. By having a good grasp of the company's financial status, firms may identify areas where cash flow may be hindered and take proactive efforts to rectify them.

Additionally, keeping solid connections with suppliers and consumers is crucial to managing cash flow properly. Negotiating advantageous payment terms with suppliers, such as extended payment periods or incentives for early settlement, may assist reduce cash flow problems. Implementing clear billing and collection methods, such as giving incentives for quick payment, may help boost cash flow.

Moreover, organizations should develop and maintain a cash reserve to manage unforeseen costs or delays in cash flow.Setting away a part of earnings into a separate account may give a safety net during hard times and provide for more flexibility in managing cash flow.

Finally, integrating technology and automation may dramatically simplify cash flow management operations. Using accounting software or cash flow management tools may assist track and analyze cash flow in real-time, offering useful insights and enabling rapid modifications as required. Automated invoicing and payment systems may help speed the payment process and increase cash flow efficiency.

In conclusion, insufficient cash flow management may be a business killer, adversely damaging the financial stability and development potential of a firm. However, by prioritizing cash flow management, properly predicting, creating solid connections, preserving cash reserves, and using technology, companies may avoid these problems and assure a healthy cash flow that supports their long-term success.

EXCESSIVE DEBT AND POOR DEBT MANAGEMENT

Excessive debt and bad debt management may be devastating to any organization, leading to a plethora of difficulties that can eventually become business killers. These flaws may impair a company's financial health, limit expansion potential, and even lead the organization to shut down totally.

One of the primary concerns linked with high debt is the pressure it causes on a company's cash flow. When a firm is laden with large levels of debt, a major amount of its monthly income is committed to paying the interest payments and principal payback. This diverts revenues away from crucial and necessary company operations such as manufacturing, marketing, and research & development. As a consequence, the organization may struggle to invest in new goods, technology, or growth, hampering innovation and competitiveness in the market.

Furthermore, high debt might produce a domino effect of financial implications. If the firm fails to pay its financial commitments, it may suffer serious penalties such as defaulting on loans or lines of credit. This not only lowers the company's creditworthiness but also puts the firm in danger of facing legal proceedings and insolvency. In such instances, the firm may find it tough to acquire future funding, hampering its capacity to recover and develop.

Poor debt management methods are another significant issue that may contribute to a company's collapse. This involves taking on debt without a realistic repayment plan, depending excessively on short-term or high-interest loans, or splurging without considering long-term effects. This lack of strategic debt management typically leads to a vicious cycle of borrowing to service current debt, resulting in a building debt load that becomes more impossible to escape.

Additionally, bad debt management may lead to a worsening relationship with creditors and lenders. Late payments or defaulting on loans may undermine a company's image and trustworthiness, making it difficult for the firm to negotiate favorable terms or receive future funding. This may be especially destructive during moments of economic downturn when firms may demand more capital to remain afloat or capture development possibilities.

Moreover, high debt and inadequate debt management may dramatically influence the morale and productivity of a company's personnel. As the financial situation worsens, there may be a need for cost-cutting measures like layoffs, compensation cutbacks, or decreased investment in staff training and development. These activities may create a toxic work atmosphere, leading to lower employee happiness, motivation, and eventually, a loss in performance.

To keep excessive debt and bad debt management from becoming business killers, firms should emphasize sensible financial planning and strategy. It is vital to thoroughly examine the risks and rewards involved with borrowing, establish a realistic repayment plan, and periodically monitor and manage the company's debt levels. This involves frequently evaluating financial accounts, following cash flow, and aggressively exploring chances to decrease debt or negotiate favorable terms with creditors.

Additionally, firms should focus on having a great connection with lenders and creditors. This entails open and clear communication, prompt payback of obligations, and a dedication to keeping a high credit score. By building trust and credibility with lenders, companies may boost their prospects of receiving advantageous financing arrangements and having access to required money when needed.

Implementing preventive financial management measures is also vital. This involves having a clear budget and monitoring costs diligently to minimize unneeded or excessive spending. By keeping a careful check on the company's financial health, firms may spot possible difficulties early on and take appropriate actions to remedy them before they become unmanageable.

Lastly, getting expert financial guidance may be important in ensuring effective debt management. Consulting with financial professionals may give organizations insights, assistance, and solutions for improving their debt management processes and lowering the danger of excessive debt.

Conclusion, high debt and inadequate debt management are substantial dangers that may seriously undermine a business's financial health and overall profitability. By emphasizing cautious financial planning, creating good connections with lenders, adopting proactive financial management procedures, and obtaining expert assistance, companies may escape the trap of excessive debt and limit the potential threats it brings. This will eventually assist organizations maintain long-term financial health, allow development prospects, and avoid becoming company killers.

IGNORING PROFITABILITY AND COST ANALYSIS

Ignoring profitability and cost analysis is a huge error that may be a company killer. Profitability is the ultimate objective for every company as it affects the success and sustainability of the endeavor. By disregarding the examination of profits and expenses, firms risk making unwise choices that may swiftly lead to financial catastrophe.

One of the key reasons to stress profitability and cost analysis is to assure long-term sustainability. Ignoring these essential aspects may result in a firm being unable to meet its expenditures, resulting in severe losses and possible insolvency. Profitability analysis helps organizations discover which goods or services are producing the most income and profit, allowing them to concentrate their efforts and resources on those areas. Similarly, cost analysis helps identify areas of wasteful spending and gives chances for cost reduction and efficiency improvement.

Moreover, profitability and cost analysis allow organizations to examine and compare their performance over time. By examining earnings and expenses, firms may uncover trends, patterns, and areas that require improvement. This research gives vital insights into the financial health of the organization and enables informed decision-making. It helps identify any possible dangers and issues that may develop and offers the chance to address them proactively.

Additionally, profitability and cost analysis offer a comprehensive picture of the business's Return on Investment (ROI). It helps organizations to identify which investments are producing the best returns and which ones are not. By neglecting this research, firms may continue investing in enterprises or projects that are not financially feasible, squandering important resources and hampering progress.

Ignoring profitability and cost analysis also leads to a lack of financial responsibility inside the firm. Without a rigorous assessment of earnings and expenditures, firms may not have a good grasp of their financial status. This lack of responsibility may result in overspending, poor resource allocation, and the inability to make educated financial choices.

Furthermore, profitability and cost analyses are vital for creating realistic pricing plans. Without knowing the costs involved in manufacturing products or services, firms risk underpricing or overpricing their offers. Underpricing reduces profitability, while overpricing may result in a loss of consumers and market share. By completing a comprehensive investigation, firms may determine optimum pricing that strikes a balance between profitability and consumer happiness.

In conclusion, disregarding profitability and cost analysis is a major error that may be a company killer. By overlooking these essential variables, organizations imperil their financial stability, ignore possibilities for growth and progress, and limit long-term success. Emphasizing profitability and cost analysis promotes wise decision-making, resource optimization, and the flexibility to respond to changing market circumstances. Hence, firms must prioritize the study of earnings and expenses to prevent the danger of becoming a business killer.

CHAPTER 3: INEFFECTIVE LEADERSHIP AND MANAGEMENT

Ineffective leadership and management may be damaging to any firm, leading to its demise and becoming a business killer. When leaders and managers fail to successfully lead and manage their teams, it generates a bad work culture, decreases employee morale, slows productivity, and ultimately hurts the overall performance of the firm.

One facet of inadequate leadership is a lack of clear direction and vision. When leaders are unable to effectively communicate corporate objectives and give a strategic direction, workers may get confused about their duties and responsibilities. This lack of clarity might result in a disengaged staff and poor production levels.

Moreover, ineffective leaders generally fail to generate a pleasant work atmosphere. They may be unable to develop open communication channels and stimulate cooperation, which is crucial for a good team dynamic. In such an atmosphere, workers are less inclined to express their concerns, exchange ideas, or contribute to the development and success of the firm. As a consequence, innovation and creativity suffer, and the firm may encounter stagnation.

Ineffective management, on the other hand, typically leads to inefficient corporate operations. Managers who lack the requisite skills or expertise may fail to successfully allocate resources, distribute duties, and monitor progress. This typically leads to delays, missed deadlines, and a lack of responsibility, producing a chaotic and unproductive office atmosphere.

Additionally, inefficient leadership and management may contribute to significant staff turnover. When leaders fail to establish a supportive and stimulating work environment, workers may feel devalued and unloved. This may lead to work unhappiness, which typically motivates brilliant people to seek better chances elsewhere. Constant turnover not only disturbs the workflow but also incurs considerable recruiting and training expenditures for the business.

Furthermore, ineffective leaders and managers generally struggle with decision-making. They may postpone or make rash judgments without contemplating the long-term effects. This indecisiveness might result in lost commercial chances or bad strategic decisions. It also weakens the faith and confidence of workers, as they begin to doubt the competency and efficacy of their leaders.

To avoid becoming a company killer, leaders and managers must have strong leadership and management abilities. Key attributes include good communication, the capacity to inspire and encourage, and the aptitude to organize and allocate duties effectively. Leaders must also build a healthy work culture focused on trust, openness, and cooperation. Investing in professional development and training programs may help leaders strengthen their abilities and remain informed about the newest trends in their sector.

In conclusion, weak leadership and management may have major ramifications for a corporation. From generating a hostile work culture to hampering productivity, it may eventually lead to the destruction of a business. To avoid becoming a business killer, leaders and managers need to acquire strong leadership and management abilities, promote a pleasant work environment, make informed choices, and emphasize the well-being and growth of their people. By doing so, executives may guide their firms toward success and assure long-term survival in an ever-changing business world.

LACK OF VISION AND DIRECTION

"Lack of Vision and Direction" is a typical business killer that may greatly limit an organization's development and profitability. When there is no clear vision for where the organization wants to go in the future and no defined course to accomplish that vision, it becomes tough to make educated choices, create objectives, and efficiently allocate resources.

Without a clear vision, workers may struggle to comprehend the purpose and goals of the firm. This lack of clarity may lead to a feeling of disengagement, as workers may not feel inspired or devoted to their tasks. Furthermore, without a clear direction, staff may have difficulties prioritizing activities, leading to inefficiencies and lost efforts.

A lack of vision and direction may also severely affect decision-making inside the firm. When there is no overall aim or plan to guide decision-making, decisions are generally made focused on short-term concerns rather than long-term possibilities. This may lead to reactive judgments, lost opportunities, and a lack of consistency in the organization's operations.

Additionally, without a clear vision and direction, it becomes tough to develop meaningful and realistic objectives. Goal-setting is a crucial component of company planning as it offers a framework for monitoring progress and success. Without a vision and direction, defining and attaining objectives becomes arbitrary and isolated from the entire corporate plan.

Allocation of resources is another area that suffers when there is a lack of vision and direction. Without a clear grasp of the organization's goals and objectives, it becomes impossible to establish where resources, such as time, money, and labor, should be spent. This may result in misallocation of resources, poor usage, and lost chances for development and innovation.

Furthermore, a lack of vision and direction may inhibit efficient communication both inside the business and with external stakeholders. A clear vision and direction create a shared purpose and language that may guide and coordinate communication efforts. When this is lacking, communications may become fragmented, inconsistent, and unclear, leading to misunderstandings, disagreements, and a breakdown in teamwork.

To avoid the business killer of missing vision and direction, firms must take proactive measures to build a clear vision for the future and construct a strategic plan to guide their activities. This entails participation in talks and brainstorming sessions to establish the organization's mission, values, and long-term objectives. Additionally, leaders should communicate the vision and direction to all stakeholders consistently and effectively, ensuring that everyone knows and is aligned with the overarching goals.

Regular evaluations and updates of the vision and strategy are also vital as company settings develop and circumstances change. This helps firms to be nimble and responsive, ensuring that they remain on track and adaptive in pursuit of their objectives. It is crucial to communicate the vision and direction across the business, ensuring that every employee knows how their tasks and duties contribute to the broader goals. This clarity helps workers to make educated judgments and prioritize duties efficiently.

By supporting a clear vision and direction, companies can inspire and engage their workers, promote innovation and development, and make informed choices that support long-term success. Avoiding the business killer of missing vision and direction is vital for developing a successful and lasting firm in today's competitive and ever-changing business world.

Finally, the absence of vision and direction may be a damaging aspect for any firm. It inhibits staff motivation, decision-making, goal-setting, resource allocation, and effective communication. To prevent this business killer, firms should have a clear vision for the future, build a strategic plan, communicate it effectively, and frequently assess and change it as required. By doing so, organizations may navigate through problems, motivate their people, and achieve long-term success.

POOR DECISION MAKING

Poor decision-making may be a big company killer and result in severe financial losses and failures. When executives and important personnel within a firm make bad judgments, it may have a trickle-down impact on all elements of the organization, leading to inefficiency, lost opportunities, and even its eventual demise.

One of the most prevalent blunders in decision-making is depending only on intuition or gut sensations without sufficient analysis and examination. While there is a benefit in following one's intuition, it is vital to obtain and evaluate relevant facts and information to make well-informed judgments. Ignoring the value of data-driven decision-making may lead to incorrect judgments and a failure to understand possible dangers and market trends that may affect the organization adversely.

Another facet of bad decision-making is a failure to explore all possibilities and alternatives. Sometimes, people prefer to cling to standard ways or approaches without seeking fresh ideas. This lack of originality and open-mindedness might restrict prospects for development and advancement, placing the organization at a disadvantage in an ever-changing commercial world. It is crucial to develop a culture that stimulates alternative thinking and celebrates new ideas to prevent slipping into the trap of bad decision-making.

Additionally, rushing into choices without sufficient preparation and research may be a devastating business killer. Impulsive decision-making typically ignores critical aspects and repercussions, resulting in bad results. It is crucial to take the time to acquire all the relevant information, engage with experts and stakeholders, and thoroughly assess the advantages and downsides before making any big choices. This rigorous approach guarantees that all possible risks and advantages are assessed, leading to more careful and informed decisions.

A lack of accountability and adequate decision-making procedures may also impede a company's performance. When choices are made without clear ownership and accountability, it becomes difficult to trace and address any negative implications. Implementing a structured decision-making framework with defined roles and duties helps to guarantee that choices are made methodically and responsibly.

Furthermore, poor decision-making might emerge from a mix of emotional connection and an inability to objectively appraise events. When people get too devoted to specific ideas or goals, they may fail to identify weaknesses or disregard competing viewpoints. Being conscious of one's prejudices and actively seeking other opinions is vital to prevent making judgments simply based on personal preferences or attachments.

To prevent the business killer of bad decision-making, it is crucial to develop a culture that stimulates critical thinking, supports data-driven analysis, and rewards innovation. Promoting a proactive attitude to decision-making ensures that risks are recognized and controlled, and opportunities are taken. Additionally, having clear decision-making procedures, such as incorporating numerous stakeholders, doing comprehensive analysis, and maintaining accountability, helps to limit the possibilities of bad decision-making.

Ultimately, bad decision-making may have significant ramifications for a corporation. It may lead to financial losses, lost opportunities, and a drop in reputation and consumer confidence. By understanding the typical dangers of bad decision-making and applying ways to prevent them, organizations may lessen the probability of falling prey to its adverse impacts and pave the road for success and development.

Remember that making incorrect judgments is a business killer. Take into consideration the significance of data-driven decision-making, evaluate all possibilities and alternatives, minimize hasty judgments, encourage responsibility, and be mindful of personal biases. By doing so, you may limit the risks associated with bad decision-making and place your organization on a road to success.

INEFFICIENT ORGANIZATIONAL STRUCTURE AND COMMUNICATION

Inefficient organizational structure and communication may be considered a company killer since it produces multiple hurdles and impediments that hamper productivity, decision-making processes, and overall effectiveness. A well-organized and efficient structure, on the other hand, is crucial for attaining the organization's goals and objectives effectively and efficiently.

One essential feature of an inefficient organizational structure is the lack of clarity in roles and duties. When team members are confused about their duties and what is expected of them, it may lead to confusion, duplication of efforts, and a lack of responsibility. This lack of clarity may also result in workers feeling alienated and detached from the organization's objective, making it harder to drive performance and achieve success.

Another consequence of an ineffective organizational structure is the silo mindset. This happens when separate departments or teams function in isolation, without adequate communication and cooperation. Silos limit the flow of information, hamper innovation, and prevent the company from using its combined expertise and resources. It also leads to internal rivalry rather than developing collaboration and cooperation, therefore squandering time, resources, and potential development prospects.

Moreover, an inefficient organizational structure might contribute to poor communication habits. Communication problems inside and between departments may result in vital information being lost or misconstrued. This leads to mistakes, delays, and misplaced objectives. Without clear and open channels of communication, workers may not have access to the information they need to make educated judgments, leading to substandard decision-making. In consequence, this might generate missing deadlines, poor customer service, and general discontent among stakeholders.

Ineffective communication also involves a lack of feedback loops. Without frequent feedback, workers may not get the required direction and assistance to enhance their performance or resolve any problems.

This may lead to frustration, demotivation, and diminished productivity.

Furthermore, an inefficient organizational structure may hamper the flow of communication between hierarchical levels. When communication is predominantly vertical and restricted to a top-down approach, key thoughts and ideas from frontline personnel or middle management may go ignored. This lack of upward communication may hinder innovation, prevent issues from being handled, and restrict the organization's capacity to adapt and change.

To prevent the business killer that is an inefficient organizational structure and communication, it is vital to emphasize clarity, alignment, and transparency. This may be done by clearly defining responsibilities and expectations, supporting cross-departmental cooperation, developing open lines of communication, and cultivating a culture of feedback and continual development. Additionally, integrating technology and digital tools may improve communication procedures, increase information exchange, and boost overall efficiency.

By addressing and resolving these organizational difficulties and investing in good communication techniques, firms may greatly enhance their operations and secure long-term success. An effective organizational structure and open communication channels offer a favorable climate for cooperation, innovation, and development, leading the way for increased production, enhanced decision-making, and happy stakeholders.

INEFFECTIVE TEAM MANAGEMENT

Ineffective team management may be a company killer if not handled swiftly and properly. When team members are not successfully managed, it may lead to a drop in productivity, poor morale, missed deadlines, and ultimately, it can damage the overall profitability of an organization.

One of the main parts of team management is ensuring that each member has a clear grasp of their duties and responsibilities. Without this clarity, misunderstanding might occur, resulting in redundancy or chores being left ignored. This lack of direction may result in workers feeling lost and unmotivated, which ultimately undermines their performance and the success of the team.

Furthermore, poor communication is another issue that leads to unsuccessful team management. When communication is inadequate, misconceptions may arise, leading to poor decision-making, redundant efforts, and a general lack of coordination among team members. Without open and transparent communication channels, team members may not feel comfortable expressing their thoughts, issues, or recommendations, impeding cooperation and creativity within the team.

Additionally, a lack of trust and support from team leaders may also contribute to inefficient team management. When leaders fail to give advice, support, and appreciation, team members may feel devalued and unloved. This might result in diminished motivation and a bad work atmosphere, ultimately harming team cohesiveness and morale. Without a cohesive team dynamic, it becomes impossible to successfully distribute duties, share responsibilities, and accomplish shared objectives.

Furthermore, inadequate team management generally neglects the value of employee development and progress. When team leaders fail to offer proper training and chances for skill growth, team members might become stagnant in their responsibilities, resulting in lost motivation and a lack of creativity. This not only hinders the individual's professional development but also impairs the general success of the team.

Moreover, a lack of recognition and incentive for strong performance might lead to inadequate team management. When team members feel underpaid and disrespected, their drive and devotion towards their task wane. This may lead to lower productivity, higher turnover rates, and an overall disengagement from the team's goals.

Ineffective team management not only inhibits the team's performance but also impacts the whole company. It may result in missing deadlines, mistakes, and low customer satisfaction. The absence of competent team management may also contribute to high turnover rates, increased absenteeism, and unfavorable business culture.

To prevent the business killer impact of inadequate team management, leaders must promote good communication, clarity in roles and duties, trust-building, and continual staff development. This may be done via frequent team meetings, clear and concise communication channels, performance reviews, mentoring programs, and team-building activities.

By putting time and effort into good team management, organizations can build a healthy and productive work atmosphere. When team members feel appreciated, encouraged, and driven, they are more likely to cooperate, innovate, and accomplish common objectives. Ultimately, good team management plays a critical role in driving the success of a firm and preventing the adverse repercussions of poor team management.

In conclusion, inadequate team management may be a company killer owing to its detrimental influence on productivity, morale, and overall performance. Firms need to emphasize successful team management by giving defined roles and duties, enabling open communication, developing trust and support, and supporting employee growth. By addressing and strengthening team management, firms may avoid the potential problems that come with inadequate management and put themselves up for long-term success.

FAILURE TO ADAPT TO CHANGE AND MARKET TRENDS

Avoiding failure to adapt to change and market trends is crucial for every company to survive and grow in today's highly dynamic and competitive world. The inability to adapt may lead to stagnation, loss of market share, and eventually, a business's extinction. Organizations need to notice and adapt to changing customer tastes, developing technology, and evolving market dynamics.

One of the biggest reasons organizations fail to adapt to change and market trends is complacency. Some firms get complacent after attaining a certain degree of success, assuming that their present strategy and practices will continue to deliver great outcomes forever. However, markets are always developing, and customer requirements and tastes are continually changing. Failing to detect and adapt to these developments might result in the firm being left behind by more inventive and adaptive rivals.

Another typical cause for the inability to adapt is resistance to change. Change may be unpleasant or upsetting, and some firms may reject change due to fear of the unknown or a desire to retain the status quo. However, refusing to accept change might impede a business's capacity to stay competitive and relevant. This reluctance may result from a lack of knowledge or awareness of the possible rewards that come with changing to market changes.

Moreover, firms that fail to react to changes and market trends generally lack flexibility and agility. They may have inflexible structures, procedures, and cultures that make them difficult to swiftly adjust to new possibilities or difficulties. These firms may be hesitant to adopt critical changes or make strategic choices owing to layers of bureaucracy or a lack of willingness to take risks. This inflexibility might hamper their capacity to pivot and adapt their business models to fit evolving trends and client needs.

The inability to adapt might also stem from a lack of foresight or market information. Businesses that do not regularly monitor and evaluate market trends may lose out on key insights and possibilities. They may fail to predict developments in customer behavior, upcoming technology, or changes in industry rules. Without a full grasp of the market environment, firms risk making choices based on obsolete or faulty information, which may lead to lost opportunities and a loss in competitiveness.

To prevent failing to adapt to change and market trends, firms need to take a proactive and forward-thinking attitude. This starts with building a culture of continual learning and innovation, encouraging people to accept change and actively seek out new ideas and viewpoints. It is vital to engage in market research and analysis to keep updated about industry trends, customer preferences, and technology breakthroughs. Regularly analyzing and updating strategies, business models, and procedures is critical to guarantee alignment with current market realities.

Additionally, firms should emphasize developing agility and flexibility in their organizational structures. This entails decentralizing decision-making, promoting cooperation across multiple departments, and allowing people to take calculated risks and react swiftly to changing conditions. By developing a culture of agility, firms may adjust rapidly to market developments and grab new opportunities as they occur.

Furthermore, firms must invest in technology and innovation to be competitive. This involves employing data analytics tools to obtain deeper insights into customer behavior, adopting automation to optimize operations, and examining upcoming technologies that may transform their sector. By adopting technology, companies may remain on the leading edge and better connect their goods and services with shifting market needs.

In conclusion, the inability to adapt to change and market trends is a typical problem that organizations must avoid to survive and prosper. Complacency, reluctance to change, inflexibility, and a lack of foresight may all lead to the failure of a firm.

By cultivating a culture of learning and innovation, being educated about market trends, adopting agility and flexibility, and investing in technology, organizations may position themselves to consistently adapt and succeed in an ever-changing business environment.

CHAPTER 4: DEFICIENT MARKETING AND CUSTOMER SERVICE

Deficient marketing and customer service may be damaging to any organization, functioning as potential "business killers." In an increasingly competitive industry, these flaws can lead to lost sales, lower customer satisfaction, and eventually, a drop in profitability.

Firstly, inadequate marketing techniques might result in organizations failing to successfully contact and engage their target audience. Without a well-defined marketing strategy, firms may struggle to build awareness and interest in their goods or services. This shortcoming might lead to a lack of lead creation and ultimately, fewer sales chances.

Moreover, bad customer service may have a substantial influence on a business's reputation and brand image. In the era of social media, consumers can readily share their experiences with a broad audience, both good and bad. When consumers find inadequate service, they are more prone to share their unfavorable experiences, possibly eroding the credibility and trust that a firm has worked hard to develop.

Furthermore, insufficient customer service might result in missed sales opportunities. Customers that get bad service are more inclined to shift their business elsewhere, seeking out rivals who value customer happiness. The expenses involved with obtaining new customers are substantially greater than maintaining current ones, making it even more vital for firms to emphasize outstanding customer service.

Additionally, weak marketing and customer service might influence a company's long-term performance and development. A lack of efficient marketing techniques inhibits a business's capacity to acquire new clients and increase its customer base. Without significant attention to customer service, firms may struggle to retain current clients and create strong, loyal relationships with them. Both of these flaws may restrict a company's total development potential and impede its capacity to stay competitive in the marketplace.

To prevent becoming a victim of these "business killers," it is vital for organizations to focus on marketing and customer service. Developing a thorough marketing strategy that incorporates a mix of conventional and digital marketing approaches can help firms efficiently reach their target audience and create leads. Employing marketing professionals or outsourcing to specialists may give significant insights and ideas for enhancing marketing efforts.

Equally vital is investing in outstanding customer service. Training personnel to deliver proactive, tailored, and timely help ensures that customers feel valued and appreciated. Implementing a customer relationship management (CRM) system may help firms manage client contacts, monitor consumer preferences, and discover areas for development.

Regularly soliciting consumer input and aggressively resolving problems or issues swiftly displays a dedication to customer happiness. Encouraging favorable online reviews and testimonials may help boost a company's reputation and attract new clients.

In conclusion, inadequate marketing and customer service may adversely damage a business's performance. By avoiding these "business killers" and adopting effective marketing techniques and outstanding customer service, companies may improve their reputation, attract and keep consumers, and eventually, achieve sustainable growth and profitability.

INADEQUATE MARKET RESEARCH AND TARGETING

Effective market research and targeting are key components of every company plan. Failing to do adequate market research or effectively identify and target prospective clients may have significant ramifications for a company's success. Inadequate market research and targeting may eventually lead to company failure. Therefore, it is necessary to devote time, money, and expertise to these areas to prevent being a business killer.

Lack of market research typically arises from a belief that it is an unneeded or time-consuming element in the company development process. However, market research gives vital insights into customer behavior, tastes, and trends. Without this information, companies are simply working in the dark, not understanding who their target audience is, what they want, or how to successfully contact them.

One of the possible consequences of poor market research is misjudging customer demand. It is vital to understand the market and its dynamics to find a feasible niche and evaluate whether there is a demand for the product or service being supplied. Overestimating or underestimating the market demand may lead to lost resources, including time, money, and effort. This may result in a substantial financial setback for a firm, which may be difficult to recover from.

Furthermore, insufficient market research may lead to poor decision-making and misdirected marketing tactics. Without a strong grasp of the target demographic, firms may struggle to express their value offer successfully or produce marketing messages that connect with their prospective consumers. This might result in low brand recognition, poor consumer engagement, and ultimately, low sales and income.

Additionally, insufficient market targeting might lead to wasteful deployment of resources. A firm that fails to define its target demographic appropriately may waste marketing expenditures in the incorrect channels or on initiatives that do not successfully reach prospective consumers. This might result in lost resources that could have been better employed to target the desired audience and achieve greater returns on investment.

To prevent these errors, organizations must emphasize market research and targeting as vital aspects of their entire strategy. It is vital to spend on obtaining data, evaluating industry trends, and knowing the target audience's requirements, interests, and habits. This may be performed via many approaches including surveys, focus groups, competitive research, and social media monitoring.

Having a good grasp of the target market helps organizations to design personalized marketing strategies, provide products or services that suit client wants, and allocate resources efficiently. The insights acquired from rigorous market research may help organizations recognize and capitalize on industry trends, build a competitive edge, and ultimately, achieve long-term success.

In conclusion, insufficient market research and targeting may have adverse impacts on a firm, possibly leading to its demise. By failing to understand the market and effectively identify and target prospective clients, firms risk misjudging demand, making bad judgments, and squandering precious resources. Investing in detailed market research and targeting is vital for organizations to build successful strategies, express their value offer, and allocate resources effectively. By avoiding the business killer of poor market research and targeting, firms may position themselves for long-term success in a competitive economy.

WEAK OR INCONSISTENT BRANDING

Weak or inconsistent branding is a big business killer that may limit development and impair a company's ability to create a loyal client base. An inadequate brand image not only fails to build awareness and recognition among consumers but also fails to deliver a clear message about what the firm stands for, making it difficult for prospective customers to comprehend and connect with the brand.

One of the main hazards of poor or inconsistent branding is the failure to distinguish from rivals. In today's crowded marketplace, companies need a unique and appealing brand identity to separate from the crowd. Without a strong brand, clients may struggle to comprehend why they should pick one firm over another, resulting in wasted opportunities and potential money.

Furthermore, uneven branding might contribute to a lack of trust and trustworthiness. When a company's branding aspects, such as logos, colors, and message, frequently change or clash with each other, consumers may see the brand as amateurish or lacking in direction. This unpredictability erodes the confidence clients invest in the brand, making it harder for them to create a lasting connection and loyalty.

Another effect of poor or inconsistent branding is the difficulty in creating brand loyalty. A successful brand establishes an emotional connection with consumers, motivating them to become committed advocates who support and promote the firm. However, if a brand fails to consistently communicate a unified and compelling message, clients may struggle to create an emotional bond or loyalty. This might result in a high customer turnover rate, since consumers may quickly migrate to rivals that have effectively created a larger brand presence.

Additionally, poor or inconsistent branding may lead to confusion and misalignment inside the organization itself. When the brand messaging is imprecise or continually changing, workers may have a hard time understanding and embracing the company's values and objectives. This lack of clarity may significantly affect employee morale, productivity, and overall corporate culture.

To avoid the business killer of poor or inconsistent branding, firms should put time and effort into building a strong and unified brand strategy. This entails precisely identifying the brand's target audience, values, and personality, as well as consistently integrating these characteristics throughout all brand touchpoints, including advertising, packaging, internet presence, and customer service.

Consistency is crucial in branding. Companies should ensure that all visual components, including logos, typefaces, and colors, stay consistent across all platforms and marketing materials. Additionally, the brand's message and tone of voice should correspond with the chosen brand personality, providing a unified and identifiable brand image.

Regularly reviewing and monitoring the brand's success is also vital. This entails obtaining input from consumers, staff, and industry experts to discover any faults or inconsistencies in the branding and make appropriate improvements. By continually refining and enhancing the brand strategy, organizations can avoid the business killer of poor or inconsistent branding and establish a powerful and identifiable brand that connects with its target audience, promotes loyalty, and generates long-term success.

NEGLECTING CUSTOMER RELATIONSHIP MANAGEMENT

In today's competitive market, customer relationship management (CRM) plays a critical part in the success of a corporation. However, many firms tend to unwittingly disregard this vital feature, threatening their existence. Neglecting CRM may have significant effects, affecting customer pleasure, loyalty, and eventually, the development of a firm. To avoid being a business killer, firms must focus and invest in creating and sustaining good customer connections.

1. Dissatisfied Customers:

When CRM is ignored, the requirements and expectations of customers are overlooked. This leads to disgruntled clients who will not hesitate to move to a rival that values and satisfies their expectations. The loss of clients not only harms current income sources but also undermines a company's reputation through unfavorable word-of-mouth, overshadowing the brand's image and reliability.

2. Decreased Customer Retention:

Neglecting CRM implies neglecting to concentrate on maintaining current clients. While recruiting new clients is crucial, retaining a loyal customer base gives stability and steady income. A lack of attention on CRM neglects the post-sales connection, resulting in consumers feeling devalued or mistreated. With greater competition, consumer loyalty is tougher to win, making retention initiatives more vital than ever.

3. Missed Revenue Opportunities:

Effective CRM helps firms to discover and grasp revenue-generating opportunities. Neglecting CRM implies not capitalizing on upselling or cross-selling chances. Without knowing consumers' desires and requirements, firms are unlikely to provide new goods or services matched with client preferences. This leads to missing revenue potential and diminished overall growth.

4. Inefficient Communication:

CRM systems allow effective contact between a firm and its clients, guaranteeing individualized interactions and fast replies. Neglecting CRM is not using such systems, resulting in chaotic and inconsistent communication. This lack of efficient communication leads to disgruntled consumers, unsolved concerns, and eventually, a decreased reputation.

5. Overlooking Customer Feedback:
CRM entails actively soliciting and absorbing consumer feedback, which is vital for continual development. Neglecting CRM implies not respecting or using customer views, losing crucial insights for product development, process refinement, and finding areas of improvement. Ignoring input inhibits a company's capacity to respond to client needs and evolving market trends, hampering corporate development.

To minimize the harmful repercussions of ignoring CRM, firms must take proactive measures:

1. Invest in CRM Technology:
Implementing uscr-friendly CRM software helps expedite customer management operations, increase communication, and promote efficiency. Invest in a sophisticated CRM system that corresponds with your business's objectives and goals.

2. Prioritize Customer Satisfaction:

Make client pleasure a key priority and instill this approach across your firm. Train staff to develop a customer-centric attitude and enable them to address client concerns swiftly and efficiently.

3. Personalize Customer Interactions:

Leverage CRM data to customize consumer interactions and create personalized experiences. Utilize client profiles and prior encounters to predict requirements and make appropriate suggestions. Small customized gestures may go a long way in developing consumer loyalty.

4. Actively Seek and Utilize Feedback:

Regularly request consumer feedback via surveys, reviews, and social media sites. Actively listen to consumer comments, resolve issues, and make required modifications based on their input. This proactive approach communicates that you appreciate your consumers' ideas and are devoted to enhancing their experience.

5. Nurture Long-term Relationships:

Establish continuing connections with your clients by keeping frequent contact, giving loyalty programs, and unique deals. Show thanks for their devotion and make them feel unique and appreciated.

Neglecting CRM might prove to be a company killer. Companies must realize and emphasize the value of creating good customer connections. By investing in CRM technology, concentrating on customer happiness, customizing interactions, actively seeking feedback, and fostering long-term connections, organizations may avoid the negative repercussions of ignoring CRM and assure sustained development and success.

INEFFECTIVE ADVERTISING AND PROMOTION STRATEGIES

Ineffective advertising and marketing techniques may be damaging to the success of any firm. These techniques fail to properly explain the value and advantages of a product or service to the target audience, resulting in low sales, wasted resources, and a bad influence on the overall reputation of the brand. It is crucial to avoid using business killer tactics to maintain the development and viability of a firm.

One of the key reasons why some advertising and marketing methods fail is the absence of sufficient market research. Without a thorough knowledge of the target audience, their wants, tastes, and habits, it becomes tough to generate a successful message and creative content that connects with prospective consumers. This frequently leads to generic and irrelevant advertising efforts that fail to catch the attention of the target market and express the unique selling proposition of the product or service.

Another typical issue is the use of obsolete or improper communication methods. With the advent of digital marketing and social media, companies need to adjust their advertising tactics to reach customers in the areas where they spend most of their time. Neglecting to exploit online platforms and neglecting to develop a strong online presence might result in lost chances to engage with prospective clients and generate leads.

Additionally, bad advertising and promotion techniques are generally characterized by a lack of consistency and regularity. Building brand awareness and recognition needs regular exposure to the target demographic. If an advertising campaign is released infrequently or lacks consistency in language and graphics, it becomes difficult for the target audience to build a clear picture of the brand and its services. This might lead to misunderstanding and disinterest, eventually limiting the profitability of the firm.

Moreover, unsuccessful advertising and promotion methods typically neglect the need of measuring and assessing campaign results. Without assessing the effect of advertising activities, it is hard to evaluate what is working and what needs improvement. Implementing analytics tools and constantly monitoring key performance indicators may give significant insights and help firms make data-driven choices to enhance their advertising and marketing campaigns.

Lastly, poor techniques tend to disregard the power of narrative and emotional connection. Consumers are not only interested in product features and specs; they want experiences and storylines that connect with their beliefs and goals. Failing to develop emotional connections with the target audience via a captivating narrative might result in a lack of engagement and a lessened capacity to catch attention amid the sea of competitor commercials.

Conclusion, inefficient advertising and promotion techniques might prove to be a company killer. Without sufficient market research, suitable communication channels, consistency, monitoring, and emotional connection, firms risk squandering money and losing out on prospective consumers. Companies must spend time and effort in designing successful advertising and marketing strategies that connect with their target demographic, leverage the correct channels, deliver a clear and compelling message, and constantly engage and resonate with customers.

By avoiding business killer techniques and employing effective advertising and promotion approaches, organizations may strengthen their brand image, attract consumers, and eventually drive growth and profitability.

CHAPTER 5: OPERATIONAL INEFFICIENCIES

Operational inefficiencies relate to procedures and processes inside a firm that are not optimized and hamper overall performance. These inefficiencies may prohibit a firm from realizing its full potential and can be damaging to its growth. To prevent these operational inefficiencies—which might be characterized as business killers—firms need to recognize, assess, and fix these problems swiftly.

One area where operational inefficiencies typically emerge is in the management of resources. When resources are not properly distributed or controlled, it may lead to waste and greater expenses. For example, if a corporation continuously overstocks goods, it locks up cash and incurs excessive storage expenditures. Conversely, inadequate inventory may lead to missed sales and harm to the company's image.

Another major operational inefficiency is insufficient communication and cooperation inside the company. When departments or teams do not successfully communicate, it may lead to duplication of efforts, delays, and misunderstandings. For instance, if the marketing department does not advise the production team about planned promotions, the production team may not be appropriately prepared, resulting in delays or blunders.

Moreover, poor technology infrastructure may also lead to operational inefficiencies. Outdated or incompatible systems may slow down procedures, restrict data flow, and impair productivity. For instance, if a corporation depends on manual record-keeping methods instead of deploying an integrated software solution, it might lead to mistakes, inefficiencies, and lost time.

Furthermore, operational inefficiencies might come from a lack of personnel training and development. When workers do not obtain the appropriate training or are not equipped with the skills and knowledge needed to do their duties successfully, it may result in mistakes, rework, and lost productivity. Investing in continual training and development programs may help staff keep up-to-date with industry trends and best practices, assuring optimum performance.

To prevent these operational inefficiencies, firms may employ many techniques. First, performing frequent audits and reviews of processes and systems may assist identify opportunities for improvement. This might entail getting input from workers, evaluating data, and comparing against industry norms. Once inefficiencies are discovered, an action plan may be designed to address and rectify these problems.

Investing in technology and automation may also assist decrease operational inefficiencies. Implementing effective software tools, such as enterprise resource planning (ERP) or customer relationship management (CRM) solutions, may expedite procedures, increase data accuracy, and boost communication and cooperation across departments.

Moreover, establishing a culture of continual improvement and innovation may prevent operational inefficiencies from repeating. Encouraging workers to submit ideas, giving chances for professional growth, and recognizing and rewarding creative solutions help build a mentality of efficiency and effectiveness inside the firm.

In conclusion, operational inefficiencies may be damaging to a firm, impeding its development and success. Firms need to detect and solve these inefficiencies immediately to avoid becoming business killers. By concentrating on resource management, efficient communication and cooperation, technology infrastructure, staff training and development, and building a culture of continuous improvement, firms may minimize operational inefficiencies and maximize their performance. Ultimately, a streamlined and effective business creates the basis for long-term success and profitability.

INEFFICIENT PRODUCTION AND OPERATIONS

Inefficient manufacturing and operations may be a business killer, presenting a danger to the existence and prosperity of any organization. These inefficiencies may result in lost production, higher expenses, and diminished customer satisfaction. Organizations need to identify and address the sources of inefficiency to avoid falling prey to this devastating problem.

One prominent reason for inefficient manufacturing and operations is inadequate management and coordination. When there is a lack of good communication, coordination, and supervision inside an organization, it may lead to confusion, duplication of efforts, and delays in output. Inefficient management methods may weaken production and hamper the overall efficiency of an organization.

Another contributing reason is a lack of optimization in manufacturing processes. When firms fail to detect and remove bottlenecks, extra procedures, and waste, it leads to reduced production and greater expenses. Inefficient processes, poorly planned layouts, and antiquated manufacturing techniques may all contribute to inefficiency in operations.

Inadequate investment in technology and infrastructure is also a big factor. Outdated equipment, software, and systems may slow down operations, increase downtime, and result in mistakes and delays. Embracing contemporary technology and investing in infrastructure improvements are vital to enhancing productivity and remaining competitive in today's fast-paced corporate climate.

Moreover, disengaged or unskilled staff may dramatically influence output and operational efficiency. When individuals lack the requisite skills, expertise, and desire to do their duties successfully, it may lead to mistakes, rework, and lost productivity.
Providing adequate training, continuous growth opportunities, and establishing a culture of employee engagement are key to enhancing efficiency and avoiding the negative effects of unproductive staff.

To avoid becoming a victim of inefficient manufacturing and operations, firms must take proactive actions to solve these difficulties. This involves doing frequent process assessments and using lean manufacturing concepts to identify and reduce waste, simplifying workflows, and improving production processes. Implementing strong management techniques, clear communication lines, and good coordination is also vital to ensure efficiency in operations.

Additionally, investment in innovative technology, equipment, and infrastructure is important to boost production. Embracing automation, digitalization, and data analytics may streamline processes, increase accuracy, and create efficiency advantages. Regularly analyzing and upgrading technology and infrastructure can help firms remain ahead and avoid the drawbacks of old systems.

In summary, inefficient manufacturing and operations may be damaging to a corporation, leading to diminished profitability and a loss of competitive edge. By addressing the causes of inefficiency and adopting proactive actions to enhance processes, invest in technology, and engage staff, companies may avoid becoming victims of inefficient production and operations and assure long-term success. Prioritizing efficiency and regularly analyzing and improving processes and systems can help organizations avoid this business killer and prosper in a competitive market.

LACK OF QUALITY CONTROL

Lack of quality control has the potential to be a huge business killer. It refers to the lack or failure of an effective system to verify that goods or services satisfy the necessary standards and specifications. Without a strong quality control strategy in place, organizations may encounter a myriad of difficulties that may dramatically influence their reputation, customer happiness, and overall success.

Firstly, a lack of quality control may result in substandard items or services being provided to clients. When organizations fail to monitor and analyze the quality of their products, they face the danger of producing goods or services that do not satisfy client expectations. This may lead to unfavorable reviews, consumer complaints, and a decreased brand image. Ultimately, it may lead clients to lose faith in the firm and to seek alternatives elsewhere, directly damaging revenue and market share.

Secondly, without quality control, a corporation can experience an increase in the amount of product recalls or service failures. Defective goods or services may not only be detrimental to consumers but can also be expensive for companies to remedy. Inefficiencies, mistakes, or safety problems might develop if quality control systems are not in place, resulting in lost time, money, and significant legal penalties. These instances may harm a company's image and may further result in legal ramifications, prospective litigation, and financial damages.

Furthermore, a lack of quality control might hamper a business's capacity to adapt and develop. Quality control methods are not just focused on discovering defects and avoiding mistakes; they also strive to identify opportunities for improvement and enhance performance. Without a quality control system, organizations may struggle to receive feedback, determine client requirements, and execute essential changes. As a consequence, they may become stagnant and fail to stay up with market developments, losing out to rivals that stress quality control and constant progress.

Moreover, a lack of quality control may significantly affect staff morale and productivity. When workers frequently experience low-quality outputs or confront impediments caused by inadequate quality control procedures, they may become demotivated and disengaged. This may lead to lower productivity, higher turnover rates, and a bad work atmosphere. Without a culture of quality control, workers may feel underappreciated and lose trust in the company's dedication to excellence.

In conclusion, the lack of quality control is a business killer. It may lead to substandard goods or services, ruin a company's image, raise expenses due to recalls or service failures, hamper innovation, and influence staff morale. Organizations must prioritize and invest in comprehensive quality control systems to guarantee that their services meet or exceed customer expectations, retain a competitive advantage, and secure their long-term success. By employing efficient quality control methods, companies may avoid the dangers of a subpar product or service, eventually boosting customer happiness, brand reputation, and overall profitability.

INADEQUATE SUPPLY CHAIN MANAGEMENT

Inadequate supply chain management may be a potential company killer if not addressed and fixed in a timely way. A well-managed supply chain guarantees that all the required materials, resources, and products are accessible and supplied effectively to fulfill client needs. Failing to do so may lead to a myriad of difficulties that can be damaging to a business's success.

One of the biggest repercussions of ineffective supply chain management is an interruption in operations. When there is a lack of coordination and control in the supply chain, it may result in delays, stockouts, and erroneous inventory levels. This might lead to clients getting their orders late or not at all, which can generate unhappiness and result in the loss of valued customers. Additionally, the failure to execute orders on time may establish a poor image for the organization, making it harder to acquire new clients and maintain current ones.

Moreover, insufficient supply chain management might lead to greater expenditures for the organization. For instance, inadequate inventory management might result in excess stock or outmoded items, tying up precious resources and cash. On the other side, stockouts might lead to urgent orders or accelerated shipment, which come with greater expenses. These extra expenditures cut into the overall profitability of the firm and undermine its competitive edge.

Inadequate supply chain management may also result in poor communication and coordination amongst different stakeholders in the supply chain. This may lead to misunderstandings, misinterpretations, and eventually, a loss of trust among partners. Without effective communication channels and coordination, it becomes tough to coordinate operations, communicate information, and make educated choices. As a consequence, the whole supply chain becomes fragmented and inefficient, limiting the smooth flow of products and services.

Furthermore, inefficient supply chain management may leave a corporation subject to different risks and interruptions. Without effective risk assessment and mitigation methods in place, any unanticipated occurrence like natural catastrophes, political instability, or changes in legislation may have serious implications on the supply chain. This might result in production delays, inventory shortages, and higher expenditures to recover from these interruptions. A lack of contingency preparations and alternate sourcing choices may further worsen the damage and make it hard for the organization to recover.

To prevent becoming a victim of weak supply chain management, firms must prioritize the creation and execution of efficient and strong supply chain procedures. This involves implementing new technology and software platforms that enable real-time visibility, data analytics, and automated procedures. It also requires developing strong relationships with suppliers, logistics providers, and other partners in the supply chain, via efficient communication and cooperation. Regular monitoring and performance review of the supply chain's key performance indicators (KPIs) may assist discover areas for improvement and ensure that the company remains on track.

Additionally, firms should engage in comprehensive risk management systems to detect and prevent possible disruptions. Incorporating a variety of resources, creating backup plans, and staying abreast of market changes and advancements are all essential components of this process. By proactively addressing possible risks and interruptions, organizations may better protect themselves from the negative repercussions of deficient supply chain management.

In conclusion, insufficient supply chain management may be a company killer if not adequately handled. It may lead to interruptions in operations, higher expenses, poor communication, and exposure to threats. To prevent these problems, firms must emphasize the creation and execution of efficient supply chain operations, embrace new technology, create teamwork, and engage in comprehensive risk management measures. By doing so, firms may streamline their supply chain, boost customer happiness, and maximize profitability.

IGNORING CUSTOMER FEEDBACK AND COMPLAINTS

Ignoring client comments and concerns may be devastating to any firm, serving as a potential killer. In today's competitive economy, customer happiness should be a key concern for firms wanting to retain a loyal client base. Neglecting consumer comments and concerns may lead to major repercussions, such as loss of revenue, harm to reputation, and loss of customer confidence.

One of the primary reasons why neglecting consumer feedback may hurt a firm is the wasted chance for progress. Customers can give important feedback about areas that require development or where the organization is falling short. By dismissing this input, firms continue to operate with defects and inefficiencies, leading to a reduction in consumer satisfaction. Over time, disgruntled clients may opt to move their business elsewhere, resulting in lost income and decreasing market share.

Moreover, disregarding consumer concerns may drastically harm a company's image. In today's linked world, unsatisfied consumers have multiple outlets to convey their unfavorable experiences, such as online review websites, social media, or word-of-mouth. Ignoring these issues displays a lack of empathy and care for consumers, which may spread swiftly and ruin a business's brand image. As prospective consumers come across unfavorable reviews, they can mistrust the company's dependability, finally opting to go for rivals instead.

Furthermore, neglecting consumer comments and concerns might diminish customer confidence. When consumers take the time and effort to submit feedback or express their problems, they want a response and resolution. By dismissing consumer advice, firms convey a clear message that customer happiness is not a priority. This may lead to a breakdown in trust and loyalty, making it more likely that consumers would seek alternatives. Trust is a delicate part of every customer-business relationship, and once it is gone, it is tough to rebuild.

To prevent these business-killing repercussions, it is crucial for organizations to actively seek out and listen to client input. Customer feedback should be considered as a chance for progress, allowing firms to address problems, make required adjustments, and enhance their products. By swiftly responding to concerns, organizations may show responsibility and a commitment to customer satisfaction. Effective customer service and complaint management may go a long way in resolving difficulties, developing trust, and keeping consumers.

Implementing a comprehensive feedback and complaint management system is vital. This might require setting up specialized channels for clients to submit feedback, such as online surveys and suggestion boxes. Regularly monitoring and evaluating consumer feedback helps discover areas for development and allows firms to take proactive steps.

In conclusion, disregarding consumer comments and complaints may be a huge business killer, leading to lost revenue, ruined reputation, and lower customer confidence. To minimize these adverse impacts, firms should aggressively seek out and listen to consumer input, immediately react to concerns, and emphasize customer pleasure.

By addressing concerns, implementing required adjustments, and showing responsibility, companies may avoid the risks associated with disregarding customer feedback and complaints and maintain a loyal and pleased client base.

CHAPTER 6: POOR RISK MANAGEMENT

Poor risk management may be a crucial element in the collapse of a corporation, as it can expose the organization to different dangers and obstacles that may finally prove deadly. Risk management refers to the process of detecting, analyzing, and minimizing possible risks to guarantee the survival and profitability of a firm. When a firm fails to adequately manage risks, it leaves itself open to several business killers that may lead to its destruction.

One of the most notable company killers coming from inadequate risk management is financial loss. A lack of risk assessment and proactive preparation may leave a firm unprepared to withstand financial setbacks such as unanticipated spending, economic downturns, or market volatility. Without suitable risk management measures in place, a firm may not have the financial buffers or contingency plans to weather the storm, ultimately leading to its collapse.

Poor risk management may also result in reputational harm, which can be a big blow to any firm. In today's linked world, news travels quickly, and negative opinions may spread like wildfire via social media and internet platforms. Failure to recognize and mitigate possible threats to a company's image might result in public scandals, customer unhappiness, or even legal concerns, inflicting permanent damage to the business's brand and status in the market.

Ignoring compliance and regulatory risks is another facet of inadequate risk management that may be disastrous to a corporation. Laws and regulations exist to enforce fair and ethical business operations, protect customers, and maintain industry standards. Failure to comply with these rules may result in large penalties, court fights, and harm to the company's reputation. Without effective risk management mechanisms in place to monitor and handle compliance and regulatory risks, a firm leaves itself open to severe repercussions, possibly leading to its destruction.

Poor risk management may also contribute to operational inefficiencies and interruptions. When a firm fails to recognize and handle operational risks, it may suffer challenges such as supply chain interruptions, technological failures, or insufficient labor management. These operational issues may limit production, interrupt the supply of products or services, and drive away consumers, eventually hurting the business's bottom line.

Lastly, inadequate risk management may hamper a company's capacity to innovate and adapt to changing market circumstances. Risk management entails spotting new trends, forecasting market upheavals, and keeping ahead of the competition. Without a proactive strategy to risk management, a company may fail to discover and capitalize on new possibilities, making it difficult for the organization to stay competitive and relevant in the long term.

Finally, inadequate risk management is a business killer that may have far-reaching implications. From financial loss to brand harm, regulatory risks to operational inefficiencies, ineffective risk management may leave a firm open to multiple dangers that might eventually lead to its destruction. Firms need to prioritize risk management and execute effective methods to detect, analyze, and mitigate risks to avoid these business killers and maintain their long-term success and resilience in the market.

INADEQUATE RISK ASSESSMENT AND MITIGATION

Risk assessment and mitigation play a key part in deciding the success or failure of enterprises. By recognizing possible dangers and devising measures to manage them, firms may secure their operations and assure longevity. However, when risk assessment and mitigation procedures are poor, firms expose themselves to a possible "business killer" that may have disastrous repercussions.

One of the key causes of ineffective risk assessment and mitigation is a lack of knowledge or comprehension of possible dangers. Companies could get complacent, thinking that since things have been going well thus far, they will continue to do so in the future. This approach might blind people to the plethora of threats hiding in the corporate environment.

Another contributing cause to insufficient risk assessment is a failure to dedicate appropriate time, money, and expertise to the process. Risk assessment needs significant study and analysis, which may be regarded as time-consuming and consequently overlooked. Additionally, committing essential resources, such as technology, manpower, or training, may appear pricey, causing organizations to underestimate the value of risk assessment and mitigation.

Furthermore, ineffective risk assessment might come from a lack of cooperation and communication inside the business. Risks frequently transcend particular divisions and influence the overall firm. Without good communication channels and cooperation across multiple departments, essential ideas and information may be ignored or not shared, resulting in a restricted awareness of possible hazards.

The repercussions of insufficient risk assessment and mitigation may be considerable and even catastrophic to an organization. Without effectively recognizing and managing risks, firms expose themselves to different hazards that may lead to financial losses, reputational harm, legal challenges, and even bankruptcy. A single occurrence or event may have a ripple effect, starting a chain reaction that paralyzes the firm and puts its existence in jeopardy.

To prevent the "business killer" caused by poor risk assessment and mitigation, firms must prioritize and invest in comprehensive risk management processes. This involves establishing a culture of risk awareness and proactively searching out possible hazards, rather than depending on reactive actions. Engaging experts or consultants in risk assessment may give important information and new viewpoints.

Allocating proper time and money for risk assessment and mitigation is critical. This includes committing employees who possess the appropriate skills to identify possible risks and devise effective measures to reduce them. It is equally crucial to harness technology and data analytics to better the knowledge of risks and assist informed decision-making.

Moreover, establishing teamwork and communication across departments is vital for a complete risk assessment. Encouraging open communication, sharing information, and engaging important stakeholders from many sectors of the company may give a more holistic perspective of risks and ensure that possible dangers are not ignored.

Regular and continuing risk assessment and mitigation actions should become part of the business's ordinary operations rather than ad hoc procedures. This enables the ongoing review and adoption of risk management techniques as the business environment develops.

Lastly, firms should also examine external variables that may affect their risk profile. Keeping a careful watch on industry developments, changes in legislation, economic swings, and geopolitical variables may assist in spot-developing risks and taking appropriate steps to manage them.

Insufficient risk assessment and mitigation might prove to be a "business killer" that inhibits the survival and development of firms. By recognizing the benefits of systematic risk assessment and investing appropriate resources, knowledge, and teamwork in the process, firms may limit possible risks and strengthen their resilience in the face of uncertainty. Taking proactive actions to mitigate risks might make the difference between long-term success and becoming a victim of weak risk management.

FAILURE TO IMPLEMENT CONTINGENCY PLANS

Failure to execute contingency measures may be a company killer. In today's ever-changing and uncertain business market, not having a sound backup plan in place may lead to severe results. Whether it's a natural catastrophe, a cyber-attack, or a worldwide epidemic, unanticipated occurrences may damage a corporation and even compel its liquidation.

One of the key reasons why failing to execute contingency planning is damaging is the possible loss of profits. When a firm is unable to continue its activities owing to unanticipated events, it cannot earn money. This lack of income may soon lead to financial distress, compromising the capacity to pay staff, and suppliers, or even cover fixed expenditures like rent or electricity. Customers may also lose faith in the firm, producing a fall in sales even after the crisis is remedied.

Another big effect of not having contingency planning is reputation harm. Customers and stakeholders want firms to be prepared and resilient in the event of hardship. Failure to plan and minimize risks might convey the appearance that a firm is unprofessional or ill-prepared, hurting its image in the market. This may be difficult to recover from since reputation is a critical motivator of consumer loyalty and trust.

A lack of contingency preparations also puts a corporation subject to competitive advantage degradation. Competitors that have contingency plans in place will be better positioned to overcome unanticipated hurdles and continue servicing their clients. This might lead to a loss of market share and competitive advantage for the firm that fails to execute contingency preparations. In today's fast-paced and highly competitive corporate climate, keeping ahead needs agility and the capacity to rapidly react to disruptions, making contingency planning an essential component of success.

Furthermore, failing to execute contingency plans might have legal and regulatory ramifications. Depending on the sector and region, firms may be subject to numerous restrictions and requirements. Failing to follow these criteria during times of crisis might result in penalties, legal action, or even license revocation. It is crucial to have contingency plans in place that meet legal and regulatory duties to prevent these potentially severe repercussions.

Ultimately, the inability to execute contingency plans may be a business killer since it raises the possibility of substantial disruptions and diminishes the odds of survival in times of crisis. Without a backup plan, a firm is at the whim of the ever-changing external environment and, as a consequence, is more prone to financial troubles, reputation harm, and loss of competitive advantage.

To avoid becoming a business killer, firms need to emphasize contingency planning as an integral element of their entire company strategy.

IGNORING LEGAL AND REGULATORY COMPLIANCE

Ignoring legal and regulatory compliance may have significant ramifications for a firm and eventually become a business killer. Compliance refers to conforming to the rules, regulations, and standards imposed by governmental organizations, industry bodies, and professional organizations.

Non-compliance may result in hefty financial fines and reputational harm. Governments and agencies have grown tougher in implementing legal and regulatory standards, so firms cannot afford to neglect them.

Here are some important reasons why neglecting legal and regulatory compliance may be bad for a business:

1. Financial Penalties: Governments impose significant fines and penalties on enterprises that fail to comply with legal and regulatory obligations. These files might vary from minor amounts to big sums, which can drastically influence a company's bottom line. The expenditures connected with legal

fights and settlements may deplete the financial resources of a corporation, possibly leading to bankruptcy.

2. Reputational Damage: Non-compliance may ruin a company's reputation. Negative publicity may stem from legal transgressions, ethical wrongdoing, or breaches of consumer privacy. The public may lose faith in the firm, leading to a loss in consumers, investors, and business partners. Rebuilding reputation and rebuilding trust is a tough and time-consuming undertaking, typically requiring major money and work.

3. Loss of Licenses and permissions: Operating a company without the proper licenses and permissions may result in closure or suspension by regulatory organizations. These licenses and permits are needed to verify that a firm fulfills specified criteria and regulations to operate lawfully. Without them, a firm may not be able to continue its activities, resulting in a stop in income creation and the loss of commercial possibilities.

4. Legal Consequences: Ignoring legal compliance may expose a corporation to litigation and legal

fights. Non-compliance may involve infractions such as infringing intellectual property rights, labor laws, consumer protection rules, environmental regulations, and health and safety standards. Lawsuits may be expensive and time-consuming, presenting a substantial danger to a business's survival.

5. Limited Growth Opportunities: Non-compliance with regulatory regulations might impede a company's capacity to grow into new areas. Many nations and areas have unique restrictions that enterprises must conform to before entering their marketplaces. Failure to achieve these standards might hinder a firm from reaching new clients and development possibilities.

6. Loss of Key Personnel: Ignoring legal and regulatory compliance may hurt staff. Violations of labor regulations or workplace safety standards may lead to high turnover rates and problems recruiting skilled personnel to the firm. Losing key individuals may interrupt corporate operations and hamper development prospects.

To avoid becoming a business killer, organizations need to emphasize legal and regulatory compliance. *Here are some actions firms should take:*

1. Stay Informed: Stay current on the newest laws, regulations, and industry standards that pertain to your firm. Regularly monitor changes in the legal and regulatory environment and ensure that your organization stays compliant.

2. Develop Compliance Programs: Establish extensive compliance programs meant to educate personnel about legal obligations, industry laws, and ethical standards. Implement rules and processes that encourage compliance across the company.

3. Provide Training: Conduct frequent training sessions for staff to increase knowledge about compliance requirements and the possible penalties for non-compliance. Training programs should concentrate on particular legal and regulatory issues important to the company.

4. Appoint Compliance Officers: Designate compliance officers or build compliance teams accountable for monitoring and enforcing

compliance inside the company. These employees should have a solid awareness of applicable rules and regulations and be enabled to take appropriate steps to preserve compliance.

5. Conduct Compliance Audits: Regularly conduct internal audits to check compliance with legal and regulatory obligations. Identify any gaps or possible areas of non-compliance and take remedial efforts to resolve them.

6. Seek Expert Advice: If required, seek legal and regulatory specialists to verify that your firm is satisfying all requirements. Legal advice may assist with complicated rules and aid with building efficient compliance plans.

7. Foster a Culture of Compliance: Instill a culture of compliance across the company by highlighting the significance of ethical behavior and legal compliance. Encourage reporting of possible non-compliance and create methods for workers to privately voice concerns.

Ignoring legal and regulatory compliance may have serious ramifications, possibly ruining a corporation.

Organizations need to realize the importance of compliance, invest in suitable systems and procedures, and prioritize adherence to legal and regulatory obligations. By doing so, firms may preserve their image, avoid financial fines, and assure sustainable development in the long term.

INADEQUATE INSURANCE COVERAGE

One of the most severe hazards to any organization is the lack of proper insurance coverage. Insufficient coverage may be hazardous to a company's existence, possibly resulting in financial collapse and lasting damage to its brand. Therefore, companies need to recognize the risks they face and ensure that they have suitable insurance coverage in place to reduce them.

The repercussions of lack of insurance coverage might be severe. In the case of an unanticipated tragedy, such as a natural catastrophe, fire, or theft, inadequate insurance coverage may leave a firm unable to recoup its losses. Without sufficient compensation, a firm may struggle to repair, replace essential assets, and continue operations, perhaps leading to a total closure.

Moreover, low insurance coverage may also hamper a business's ability to meet its legal duties. Many sectors and countries require organizations to carry certain insurance plans, such as workers' compensation or liability insurance. Failing to follow these regulatory standards may result in expensive penalties, legal ramifications, and ruined relationships with stakeholders.

Furthermore, reputation harm might be a serious consequence of a lack of insurance coverage. If a firm is unable to meet its promises to clients, customers, or workers owing to inadequate coverage, its reputation may be irreversibly tarnished. In today's digital environment, news travels swiftly, and bad publicity may spread like wildfire. This might lead to a loss of confidence among present and future customers, partners, and investors, affecting the business's ability to attract new prospects and flourish.

To avoid being subject to the business killer of insufficient insurance coverage, organizations need to take proactive actions toward complete risk management.

Here are a few major considerations:

1. Risk Assessment: Conduct a comprehensive examination of all possible hazards your organization may face. This involves analyzing possible hazards to physical assets, liability risks, business disruptions, employee well-being, and cyber dangers, among others. Understanding your risks will assist establish the appropriate insurance coverage.

2. Seek Professional Advice: Consult with insurance specialists that specialize in your sector to assist identify possible hazards and advice on the most suitable insurance coverage. Insurance brokers or risk management consultants may give experienced help in choosing policies that correspond with your company objectives and reduce particular risks.

3. Regularly assess and Update Policies: organization dynamics vary over time, so it is vital to assess insurance coverage regularly to ensure it currently effectively covers your organization. As

your company expands or launches new goods or services, the insurance coverage should be evaluated to meet the changing demands.

4. Maintain Adequate Coverage Limits: Ensure that the coverage limits of your insurance products are adequate to cover any losses. Underinsurance may be as damaging as having no insurance at all. Calculate the possible expenses associated with various hazards and make sure your plans offer appropriate protection.

5. Consider Additional Coverages: Depending on your sector and individual hazards, there may be specialty insurance plans that may give additional layers of protection. For example, cybersecurity insurance may assist defend your firm from data breaches and cyber-attacks.

6. Keep Records and Documentation: Maintain complete records of all insurance policies, premiums, and claims. This will assist guarantee that you have an accurate picture of your coverage and speed up the claims procedure in case of an occurrence.

7. Training and Education: Invest in training programs to educate personnel about risk management and the need for insurance coverage. This will assist build a culture of risk awareness and ensure that everyone knows their responsibility in minimizing possible dangers.

Inadequate insurance coverage might be a company killer, but it is not an insurmountable obstacle. By taking early efforts, frequently evaluating and revising policies, and getting expert guidance, organizations may protect themselves against financial disaster, legal penalties, and reputational harm. Prioritizing proper insurance coverage will allow organizations to concentrate on development, innovation, and long-term sustainability.

CHAPTER 7: IGNORING TECHNOLOGY ADVANCEMENTS

Ignoring technological improvements may be a big drawback for firms, ultimately leading to stagnation and finally being a company killer. In today's fast-paced digital world, technology plays a key role in every element of the company, from operations to marketing to customer service. Failing to adopt, adapt, and exploit technology may have adverse repercussions on a company's competitiveness and overall performance.

One of the key reasons why disregarding technological improvements might adversely affect a firm is the missing chances for efficiency and productivity advantages. With each passing year, new technology solutions emerge that may automate and simplify numerous company operations, saving time, cutting expenses, and enhancing overall efficiency. Companies that choose to disregard these innovations risk becoming inefficient, outmoded, and unable to stay up with their rivals who have adopted new technology.

Ignoring technological improvements may also limit a business's ability to connect and interact with its target audience efficiently. The development of the internet and social media platforms has radically transformed the way customers engage with companies and make purchase choices. Businesses that refuse to implement digital marketing tactics and technologies may struggle to engage with their target audience, eventually losing market share to more tech-savvy rivals.

Moreover, disregarding technological improvements might significantly affect client happiness and loyalty. Today's consumers have grown to demand seamless, tailored experiences across numerous channels, both online and offline. Technologies such as customer relationship management (CRM) systems, chatbots, and data analytics allow organizations to acquire important information about their consumers, tailor their interactions, and deliver great customer service. By disregarding these improvements, firms risk alienating their consumers and losing their allegiance to rivals who can satisfy their shifting expectations.

In addition to consumer happiness, cybersecurity is another crucial issue that firms cannot afford to overlook. As technology continues to improve, so do the challenges to data security. Ignoring developments in cybersecurity safeguards may leave a corporation exposed to cyberattacks, data breaches, and loss of critical information. These occurrences not only hurt a company's image but may also lead to legal ramifications and financial loss.

Lastly, failure to accept technological improvements may also impede a business's capacity to recruit and retain top employees. In today's work market, tech-savvy professionals with talents in areas such as data analysis, artificial intelligence, and cloud computing are highly sought after. By rejecting technology improvements, organizations risk being viewed as antiquated and uninteresting to prospective workers who value working in creative, forward-thinking workplaces.

Finally, disregarding technological improvements may have significant ramifications for firms, leading to inefficiency, lost competitiveness, consumer unhappiness, cybersecurity threats, and issues hiring top people. It is vital for companies to keep educated and adaptive, continually reviewing and incorporating current technology to enhance their operations, communicate with consumers efficiently, and stay ahead in the market. By adopting digital innovations, organizations may position themselves for growth, success, and longevity.

FAILURE TO EMBRACE DIGITAL TRANSFORMATION

Avoiding digital transformation in today's quickly developing business world is similar to accepting a death sentence for any corporation. The refusal to embrace digital transformation might prove to be one of the greatest business killers, resulting in stagnation, loss of competitive advantage, and eventually, collapse.

Digital transformation is the process of infusing digital technology into every area of corporate operations, including consumer engagement, operational procedures, and business models. It entails utilizing the power of technology to simplify operations, increase efficiency, enhance customer experience, and reinvent current goods or services. However, many companies remain averse to change, fearing the risks and disruptions that come with digital transformation. Unfortunately, this worry might prove to be destructive in the long term.

One of the biggest repercussions of failing to embrace digital transformation is falling behind the competition. In today's fast-paced and digital-centric environment, consumers have grown to demand flawless and efficient online experiences. Failure to achieve these expectations may leave firms struggling to retain consumers. Competitors that have effectively adapted to digital transformation will get an upper hand, giving better online experiences and more convenient services, therefore attracting and maintaining the consumer base.

Moreover, failure to embrace digital transformation inhibits corporate agility and creativity. Digital technologies give firms with significant data insights, allowing them to make data-driven choices and identify new possibilities or holes in the market.

By delaying digital transformation, organizations lose out on using the potential of data analytics, artificial intelligence, and automation to streamline operations, enhance decision-making, and drive innovation. This lack of adaptability may result in inefficient operations, obsolete business models, and an inability to respond to changing client wants or market trends.

Another key feature of digital transformation is the capacity to reach a bigger audience and develop a market presence. With the expanding popularity of e-commerce and the increasing dependence on digital channels for information and purchases, firms that refuse to embrace digital transformation restrict their reach and lose out on prospective clients from across the world. This constrained market presence might impair development possibilities and reduce revenue production.

Furthermore, not adopting digital transformation may lead to greater expenses and inefficiencies. Digital technologies provide several cost-saving advantages, such as automation of repetitive processes, enhanced supply chain management, and optimum resource allocation. By opposing these improvements, organizations may continue to depend on manual procedures and outmoded technologies, resulting in inefficiencies, higher expenses, and lost profitability.

Failing to embrace digital transformation is a huge business killer in the current day. It inhibits competition, reduces market presence, limits innovation, and raises expenses. Embracing digital transformation is no longer a luxury but a need for enterprises to survive and prosper. It demands a proactive attitude, a willingness to adapt, and a systematic strategy to integrate digital technology into every part of the organization. By doing so, firms may unleash new possibilities, improve consumer experiences, streamline processes, and safeguard their place in an increasingly digital environment.

INADEQUATE IT INFRASTRUCTURE AND SUPPORT

One of the important criteria for the success of any firm is its capacity to efficiently employ information technology (IT) infrastructure and obtain trustworthy assistance. In today's digital era, firms largely depend on IT systems for different activities, such as data storage, communication, and process automation. However, poor IT infrastructure and support may become a business killer, hurting productivity, efficiency, and even profitability.

Firstly, a poor IT infrastructure may significantly hinder a company's capacity to execute its regular activities successfully. Slow and obsolete hardware and network systems may cause delays, bottlenecks, and unresponsive software, restricting workers from accomplishing their responsibilities properly. This might result in lower productivity, missing deadlines, and unsatisfied consumers or clients.

Moreover, an inadequate infrastructure may lack the essential backup and security safeguards, exposing the organization to possible data breaches, loss, or corruption. These may have major legal and financial ramifications, hurting the business's brand and trustworthiness.

Additionally, the absence of effective IT assistance exacerbates the negative effects of insufficient infrastructure. When technological difficulties develop, staff need rapid support to remedy the problems and minimize downtime. Without a specialized and timely IT support team, the organization may endure protracted service interruption, resulting in dissatisfied workers and decreasing customer satisfaction. Furthermore, without proactive maintenance and monitoring, possible faults may go undiscovered and unsolved, raising the risk of system failures or cyberattacks.

Inadequate IT infrastructure and support may also limit a company's capacity to adapt and innovate in today's continuously changing business environment. Outdated technology and lack of support for rising innovations, such as cloud computing or artificial intelligence, may put a corporation at a major disadvantage compared to rivals.

Modern IT infrastructure and support are vital for installing new software or tools, allowing effective communication, and keeping ahead of market trends. A firm that fails to invest in its IT infrastructure and support may struggle to keep up with the growing market needs and technological improvements, resulting in lost opportunities and loss of competitive advantage.

Furthermore, poor IT infrastructure and support may have an adverse influence on staff morale and satisfaction. Frustration with sluggish systems, frequent technological failures, and inattentive assistance may lead to demotivated and disengaged personnel. When workers do not have the required tools and assistance to execute their duties successfully, their job satisfaction declines, leading to lower productivity and increasing turnover rates. This might create a poor work atmosphere and damage the overall performance of the organization.

To avoid becoming a business killer, firms must prioritize investing in dependable and up-to-date IT infrastructure and support. Regular evaluations, updates, and proactive maintenance should be undertaken to ensure that hardware, software, and network systems are capable of fulfilling the business's demands. Additionally, having a dedicated IT support staff or outsourcing IT services may guarantee that technological problems are immediately resolved, limiting downtime and delays.

Moreover, organizations should keep updated about technical developments and market trends to find chances for utilizing IT infrastructure to promote innovation and acquire a competitive advantage. This may entail studying cloud computing, adopting agile development approaches, or deploying sophisticated cybersecurity measures.

Lastly, building a culture of continual learning and IT literacy among workers may considerably help to leverage the advantages of IT infrastructure. Providing training and tools to workers may empower them to efficiently use technology and prevent possible difficulties on their own, lowering the pressure on IT assistance.

In conclusion, poor IT infrastructure and support may be a business killer, slowing productivity, inhibiting adaptation, and harming staff morale. To prevent this, organizations must acknowledge the necessity of investing in solid IT infrastructure, proactive support, and being up-to-date with developing technology. By doing so, businesses can assure seamless operations, stimulate innovation, and preserve a competitive advantage in today's digital market.

NEGLECTING CYBERSECURITY MEASURES

In today's technologically savvy world, organizations are increasingly depending on digital platforms to store and manage their important information. From client data to proprietary technology, this digital ecosystem brings both possibilities and difficulties. One key concern that firms sometimes overlook to handle appropriately is cybersecurity protection.

Neglecting cybersecurity precautions may be damaging to any organization, ultimately becoming a possible business killer. The repercussions of failing to prioritize cybersecurity may have far-reaching effects, including financial losses, brand harm, legal challenges, and even the entire closure of the firm.

First and foremost, disregarding cybersecurity enables fraudsters to exploit holes inside a business's digital infrastructure. These thieves are tenacious in their pursuit of valuable data, aiming to steal critical information or destroy operations. Once compromised, firms may experience financial losses, such as direct losses from stolen cash or indirect losses arising from interrupted operations. The expense of recovering from such assaults may be high, frequently resulting in diminished profitability or even insolvency.

Moreover, the consequence of a cybersecurity attack goes beyond financial losses. Reputational damage is a serious consequence that organizations confront when their consumers' trust is undermined. News of a security breach may spread swiftly, resulting in a loss of consumer trust and loyalty. Customers may opt to move their business elsewhere, resulting in a reduction in revenue and market share. Rebuilding a shattered image is not an easy undertaking and may require a substantial amount of time and money.

Legal issues can emerge when cybersecurity measures are overlooked. Businesses are generally subject to numerous rules and compliance requirements, depending on their industry. Failing to adopt proper cybersecurity safeguards may lead to infractions of these standards, resulting in legal penalties, fines, and litigation.

Moreover, corporations may be held accountable for any damages or losses experienced by their customers or business partners as a consequence of a cybersecurity breach. This may further drain financial resources and even ruin the firm.

Lastly, disregarding cybersecurity precautions might eventually lead to the downfall of an organization. With the rising frequency and complexity of cyber attacks, investors and stakeholders are increasingly more aware of a business's capacity to defend its assets. If a corporation has a track record of bad cybersecurity procedures, it may struggle to recruit investors or partners, resulting in a loss of capital and development possibilities. In severe circumstances, organizations that repeatedly disregard cybersecurity may face regulatory punishment or forced shutdowns.

To prevent becoming a victim of these potential economic killers, firms must prioritize cybersecurity safeguards. Implementing strong security measures, routinely upgrading software, performing risk assessments, and teaching personnel about cybersecurity best practices are key tasks. Additionally, investing in cybersecurity technology and working with respected cybersecurity organizations may give extra levels of safety.

In conclusion, disregarding cybersecurity measures is a severe error that no organization can afford to make. The implications may be serious, ranging from money losses to reputational harm and legal concerns. To avoid becoming a business killer, firms must prioritize cybersecurity measures and actively strive towards developing a robust and durable digital infrastructure. By doing so, companies may preserve their precious assets, retain consumer trust, and assure their long-term survival and development in an increasingly digital environment.

CHAPTER 8: WEAK SALES AND REVENUE GENERATION

Weak sales and revenue production may be damaging to any company since it directly affects the entire profitability and sustainability of the firm. Organizations must detect and solve this problem early to avoid encountering substantial hurdles or even failure.

One of the primary causes for inadequate sales and income creation may be ascribed to an inefficient or insufficient marketing strategy. If a firm fails to connect with its target market or fails to properly explain the value proposition of its goods or services, sales are likely to suffer.

Firms must undertake extensive market research, discover the requirements and preferences of the target audience, and customize their marketing activities appropriately. By designing an engaging marketing plan, firms may create more leads and attract new consumers, ultimately improving sales and income.

Furthermore, a lack of innovation and product development may also lead to inadequate sales and income growth. In today's highly competitive business world, it is vital for organizations to consistently innovate and deliver new and better goods or services to fulfill the ever-changing wants of customers. Failure to do so might result in the loss of market share and income. Businesses should engage in research and development operations, listen to consumer input, and always seek to enhance their services to be relevant and competitive in the market.

Another aspect that might lead to inadequate sales and income development is the subpar client experience. Providing an amazing customer experience is crucial for companies to establish loyalty, boost customer happiness, and ultimately drive sales. If consumers have a bad experience with a company, such as poor customer service, delayed response times, or insufficient product quality, they are unlikely to make repeat purchases or promote the firm to others. Therefore, firms should invest in offering customized and prompt customer service, maintaining product quality and dependability, and consistently seeking input to enhance the entire customer experience.

In addition to these elements, economic volatility, market saturation, and external events such as pandemics or political instability may also affect sales and income creation. While firms may not have complete control over these issues, implementing agile tactics and diversifying income sources may help reduce the negative consequences. For instance, organizations might explore new markets, build strategic relationships, or engage in online platforms to broaden their reach and tap into other client categories.

To minimize the harmful effects of inadequate sales and revenue production, organizations must emphasize the adoption of successful sales and marketing strategies, product innovation, offering excellent customer experiences, and being responsive to external circumstances. By regularly monitoring key performance indicators, finding areas of development, and swiftly resolving any difficulties, organizations may boost their sales and income creation, assuring long-term success and sustainability.

It is also vital for organizations to regularly review the efficiency of their sales and income production methods. Regularly examining sales procedures, monitoring market trends, and assessing client feedback may give useful insights into areas that need improvement. This helps organizations make required modifications, enhance their strategy, and remain ahead of the competition.

Finally, firms must emphasize excellent financial management techniques to minimize future revenue shortages and offset the negative impacts of lower sales. This involves keeping accurate financial records, managing cash flow properly, and adopting cost-saving measures as appropriate. By regularly monitoring and managing finances, firms may guarantee they have the means to weather any downturns in sales and income and sustain corporate operations.

In conclusion, insufficient sales and revenue development might be a huge company killer. However, by identifying the elements that lead to such issues and adopting proactive actions to overcome them, organizations may prevent the detrimental effect on their overall performance and sustainability. From executing efficient marketing tactics to promoting innovation and providing excellent customer experience, organizations must continually seek to strengthen their sales and income production skills. By doing so, companies may not only survive but also prosper in a highly competitive environment.

INEFFECTIVE SALES STRATEGIES

In the fast-paced world of commerce, sales techniques play a critical part in driving the success of a corporation. A well-executed sales plan may lead to greater revenue, market share growth, and better brand visibility. On the other side, an inefficient sales strategy might become a business killer, compromising the whole organization's future. Firms need to detect and improve any unsuccessful sales methods swiftly to prevent falling prey to this feared result.

One of the most frequent errors that firms confront is having an unsuccessful sales plan. This happens when firms fail to adapt to changing market dynamics, disregard client wants, or depend on obsolete sales strategies. To prevent the business killer, it is vital to spot the indicators of an inefficient sales strategy and take quick actions to fix the issue.

One symptom of an inadequate sales strategy is a drop in sales performance or stagnation in revenue growth. This might signal that the present strategy is no longer connecting with the intended client base or failing to satisfy shifting market needs. It is vital to routinely examine sales data and KPIs to spot any concerning patterns and take proactive efforts to change the sales strategy appropriately.

Another prominent symptom of an inefficient sales approach is high client turnover or poor customer retention rates. This shows that the present technique could be failing to fulfill client expectations or deliver adequate value. Conducting customer surveys or requesting feedback directly from customers may give useful insights into their satisfaction levels and help identify areas of development.

Additionally, unsuccessful sales methods typically disregard the necessity of creating good connections with clients. Relationships are the cornerstone of effective sales, and neglecting to invest in them may be damaging to long-term success. Building trust, delivering tailored solutions, and keeping a constant connection with customers are all critical parts of a great sales approach.

Furthermore, a lack of flexibility might make a sales plan unproductive. In today's quickly shifting market, companies need to remain ahead of the curve and consistently change their strategy to meet new problems and possibilities. Failing to accept new technology, trends, or client preferences might impede a company's capacity to prosper in the competitive market.

To avoid the business killer of an inefficient sales strategy, firms must be ready to spend on continual training and development of their sales personnel. Equipping salespeople with the required skills, information, and resources to succeed is vital for the execution of a successful sales plan.

In conclusion, an unsuccessful sales strategy may constitute a substantial danger to the profitability and longevity of an organization. Recognizing the indicators of an unsuccessful strategy, such as poor sales performance, high customer attrition rates, and a lack of flexibility, is vital for avoiding the business killer. By routinely assessing sales data, getting consumer input, creating strong customer connections, and remaining adaptive in the face of change, firms may fix failed sales techniques and position themselves for continuous development and success.

LACK OF SALES TRAINING AND MOTIVATION

The absence of sales training and motivation may be a damaging feature for any firm, frequently failing to accomplish targeted sales objectives and overall success. Ignoring or overlooking the significance of training and motivating sales personnel may have significant effects, which is why organizations need to prioritize these areas if they desire to avoid being company killers.

Sales training plays a key role in preparing sales professionals with the essential skills, information, and tactics needed to efficiently close transactions and produce money. Without sufficient training, salespeople may fail to grasp the qualities and advantages of the items or services they are selling, resulting in an inability to properly connect with prospective consumers. This lack of understanding may directly affect the sales process, resulting in missed opportunities and lower income.

Furthermore, a lack of sales training sometimes leads to uneven sales tactics across the firm. Each salesman may approach prospective customers differently or fail to follow a consistent sales procedure, resulting in confusion and a lack of coherence among the team. Inconsistent processes not only make it harder to monitor success but also harm the general reputation and image of the organization. Untrained sales personnel may unwittingly deliver false information or fail to handle customer problems appropriately, leading prospective customers to lose confidence and turn elsewhere for their requirements.

In addition to training, motivation is equally crucial to achieve sales success. Without sufficient motivation, sales teams may lack the drive and excitement required to continually put up their best efforts. A lack of motivation may be depressing for salespeople, leading to lower productivity, diminished confidence, and eventually, lost sales.

Motivation may come in different ways, including recognition, awards, and incentives. Recognizing and appreciating the efforts and successes of salespeople may go a long way in increasing their morale and drive. Setting reasonable objectives and giving concrete prizes for attaining or surpassing targets may also act as potent motivators. Incentives such as commission schemes or incentives may give the essential motivation for salespeople to go above and beyond, creating sales success for the firm.

A firm that fails to give sales training and incentive runs the danger of not just losing prospective sales but also losing valued salespeople. Untrained and demotivated sales personnel may become disillusioned and disengaged, seeking chances elsewhere with firms that value their development and success. This turnover may be expensive for firms, both in terms of recruiting and lost knowledge and skills.

To avoid becoming a company killer, organizations need to invest in sales training and motivation.

Providing thorough training programs that concentrate on product knowledge, sales skills, and effective communication helps provide sales personnel with the required tools to flourish in their professions. Regular coaching sessions, seminars, and continuous training may also assist refine their abilities and keep them up to speed with industry trends.

Similarly, developing a comprehensive incentive plan is vital to keep salespeople motivated and focused. This might entail establishing a happy work atmosphere, promoting a culture of recognition and appreciation, and delivering appealing incentives and rewards. Regular contact and feedback with sales professionals are also crucial to understand their issues, solving their concerns, and giving the required assistance.

By emphasizing sales training and motivation, organizations can empower their sales staff to perform at their best, meet sales objectives, and contribute to overall company success. Failure to invest in these important areas may impair sales success, lead to lost revenue, and eventually, become a company killer. Therefore, firms must realize the value of sales training and motivation and make them important components of their development plan.

POOR PRICING STRATEGY

A bad pricing strategy may be a huge business killer, leading to lower profitability, diminished market share, and even the eventual demise of a corporation. Pricing is a vital part of every organization since it directly influences consumer perception, competition, and ultimately, the bottom line. When a firm fails to establish an effective pricing strategy, it may have disastrous effects.

One of the most frequent errors that companies make is establishing pricing too low. While it may seem contradictory, selling items or services too cheap may hurt a firm in various ways. Firstly, it decreases the perceived value of the item, making clients doubt its quality or usefulness. Consequently, shoppers could select higher-priced rivals as they feel they give more value for money.

Additionally, pricing prices too low may not produce sufficient income to pay expenditures, leading to financial instability and ultimate company collapse.

On the other hand, establishing prices too high might also be damaging. Customers are more price-sensitive and value-conscious, and they have access to various alternatives in the market. If a firm overpriced its goods or services, it could struggle to attract consumers and lose market share to rivals providing identical things at cheaper costs.

This will not only impact current sales but may also damage the firm's image in the long term, making it A bad pricing strategy that can be a huge business killer, leading to lower profitability, lost market share, and even the eventual demise of a corporation. Pricing is a vital part of every organization since it directly influences consumer perception, competition, and ultimately, the bottom line. When a firm fails to establish an effective pricing strategy, it may have disastrous effects.

One of the most frequent errors that companies make is establishing pricing too low. While it may seem contradictory, selling items or services too cheap may hurt a firm in various ways. Firstly, it decreases the perceived value of the item, making clients doubt its quality or usefulness. Consequently, shoppers could select higher-priced rivals as they feel they give more value for money. Additionally, pricing prices too low may not produce sufficient income to pay expenditures, leading to financial instability and ultimate company collapse.

On the other hand, establishing prices too high might also be damaging. Customers are more price-sensitive and value-conscious, and they have access to various alternatives in the market. If a firm overpriced its goods or services, it could struggle to attract consumers and lose market share to rivals providing identical things at cheaper costs. This will not only impact immediate sales but may also damage the business's image in the long term, making and failing to appropriately analyze expenses can contribute to a bad pricing plan.

To prevent this business killer, organizations need to devote time and money to building an efficient pricing strategy that incorporates all these aspects. Regular examination, modification, and being alert to market developments may assist guarantee that a firm retains a competitive advantage, optimizes profitability, and avoids the drawbacks of a bad pricing plan.

INADEQUATE SALES FORECASTING AND PIPELINE MANAGEMENT

Inadequate sales forecasting and pipeline management may be a company killer if not adequately handled. This vital part of corporate operations covers the projection of future sales and the proper management of possible leads and prospects. Failing to estimate properly and manage the sales funnel may result in missed sales objectives, revenue loss, and ultimate company collapse.

One of the key disadvantages of weak sales forecasting is the failure to deploy resources properly. Without a good picture of future sales, a firm may overinvest in inventory or manufacturing capacity, resulting in excessive costs and a possible cash flow problem. On the other side, underestimating sales might lead to lost possibilities for growth, since the firm may not be well prepared to fulfill client demand.

Furthermore, poor sales forecasting may also compromise a company's capacity to make educated strategic choices. Executives and managers depend on accurate sales predictions to make key decisions regarding product development, establishing sales objectives, allocating funds, and organizing marketing campaigns. Without precise estimates, these judgments might be based on guesswork or inadequate information, which raises the risk of making expensive errors.

Additionally, inefficient pipeline management may result in wasted sales opportunities and lower customer satisfaction. A badly managed sales pipeline implies insufficient follow-up on leads, longer sales cycles, and higher possibilities of transactions slipping through the cracks. It is crucial to have a well-defined strategy for managing the pipeline, including frequent monitoring, nurturing leads, and giving timely and appropriate information to prospective consumers. Failure to do so might result in prospects losing interest, feeling dissatisfied, or selecting a rival who has greater communication and involvement.

Inadequate sales forecasting and pipeline management also lead to poor financial performance. A corporation that cannot effectively estimate its sales and manage its pipeline may fail to reach revenue objectives and sustain continuous cash flow. This may lead to a range of financial concerns, including rising debt, trouble accessing funding, and probable layoffs or downsizing.

To avoid the hazards of insufficient sales forecasting and pipeline management, firms should invest in solid systems and procedures that allow accurate forecasting and successful pipeline management. This may require integrating sophisticated analytics tools, educating sales personnel on best practices, and frequently analyzing and updating projection models and pipeline indicators. It is vital to employ technology to collect and analyze sales data, spot patterns, and alter plans appropriately.

Moreover, developing teamwork between the sales, marketing, and finance departments is vital. By coordinating these divisions and establishing a feedback loop, a firm may increase sales forecasting accuracy and guarantee that all teams are working towards shared objectives. Regular communication and data sharing across these departments may give significant insights into customer behavior, market trends, and competition positioning, which can boost the accuracy of sales forecasting and pipeline management.

In conclusion, bad sales forecasting and pipeline management may be damaging to a business's performance. It may lead to financial instability, lost opportunities, and poor decision-making. To prevent these risks, firms must emphasize accurate sales forecasting and invest in robust pipeline management procedures. By doing so, businesses may optimize resource allocation, make informed strategic choices, maximize sales prospects, and eventually achieve sustainable development.

CHAPTER 9: NEGLECTING HUMAN RESOURCES

In today's hyper-competitive business market, firms must be alert and proactive in managing every area of their operations. While many firms concentrate on raising revenue, gaining market share, or embracing new technology, they frequently forget the important aspect of human resources. Neglecting the management and development of people may eventually lead to serious repercussions and even become a company killer.

Human resources play a critical role in building a great work culture, attracting top talent, offering training and development opportunities, and guaranteeing employee happiness. Ignoring these principles might result in numerous adverse repercussions for a corporation.

One of the most serious repercussions of ignoring human resources is a high employee turnover rate. Employees who feel underpaid, unloved, or missing development prospects are inclined to consider other job possibilities. This may lead to a revolving door of personnel, severely influencing team chemistry, production, and the overall profitability of an organization.

Furthermore, a firm that disregards human resources is prone to suffering a reduction in production and performance. Employees who do not get enough training or assistance may struggle to reach the expectations set for them, resulting in lower production and lost opportunities. Additionally, a lack of efficient communication routes and feedback systems may hamper cooperation and hinder creativity inside an organization.

Moreover, disregarding human resources may have an adverse influence on employee morale and happiness. When workers feel unvalued or unheard, their passion, energy, and devotion to the business decline. This may result in diminished engagement, poor job satisfaction, and ultimately a hostile work environment. Such unfavorable conditions may further accelerate turnover, as well as ruin the image of the organization, making it harder to recruit and retain top people.

Another business killer associated with ignoring human resources is the possibility of legal and ethical concerns. Failing to give sufficient training on subjects such as harassment prevention, discrimination, and privacy rules may expose a corporation to litigation and reputational harm. Negligence in keeping personnel records, processing payments, or neglecting labor rules may lead to significant legal implications.

To prevent these dangers, firms must prioritize their people's resources. They should invest in recruiting **HR** specialists who can efficiently handle employment-related concerns, establish and execute training programs, and create a healthy work environment. These personnel should be educated to recognize and resolve possible difficulties before they become serious problems. Regular employee feedback surveys, performance assessments, and professional development opportunities should also be part of a complete human resources plan.

Furthermore, a significant focus on communication and employee appreciation is vital. Regular team meetings and town hall sessions may offer workers a forum to vent their issues, discuss ideas, and feel appreciated. Implementing recognition programs, awards, and incentives may help enhance staff morale and motivation.

In conclusion, disregarding human resources might prove to be a company killer. Organizations that fail to focus on the management and development of their personnel face high turnover rates, poor productivity, employee unhappiness, legal challenges, and bad work culture. By investing in human resources and building a supportive and empowering environment for workers, organizations may increase their position in the market, attract top talent, and ultimately secure long-term success.

LACK OF PROPER HIRING AND SELECTION PROCESS

The absence of a competent recruiting and selection procedure is a major problem that may become a potential company killer. In today's extremely competitive business world, firms require smart and competent personnel who can contribute successfully towards accomplishing their objectives. However, without a comprehensive recruiting and selection procedure in place, firms are in danger of making incorrect judgments that may eventually have fatal effects.

One of the key reasons why the lack of a thorough recruiting and selection process may be damaging to a company is the danger of employing the incorrect employees. Human resources are a company's most precious asset, and employing the incorrect individual may have a detrimental influence on the overall productivity, team chemistry, and ultimately, the bottom line. An inappropriate recruit may lack vital skills, have a bad work ethic, or show toxic conduct, which may drastically disrupt the company's operations and destroy its image.

Additionally, a lack of adequate recruiting and selection procedures might lead to a mismatch between the candidate's credentials and the job requirements.
A corporation that fails to appropriately analyze a candidate's abilities, experience, and cultural fit with the organization may find itself with personnel who are ill-suited for their jobs. This may result in a high employee turnover rate since unsatisfied or underperforming workers are more inclined to depart.

Not only does this cause instability within the workforce, but it also incurs extra expenditures for recruiting, onboarding, and training new personnel.

Furthermore, a lack of a structured recruiting and selection procedure might open the doors to biased decision-making. Unconscious biases may obscure judgment and limit the selection of the best individuals based simply on their skills and talents. This may lead to a homogenous workforce that lacks variety and creativity, thus hampering the company's capacity to adapt to new problems and capitalize on emerging possibilities.

Without a thorough recruiting and screening procedure, organizations may potentially face legal concerns. Discrimination lawsuits might occur if applicants believe they were neglected owing to criteria such as their color, gender, age, or handicap. Such litigation may destroy a company's reputation, harm its brand image, and result in significant legal fees and settlements.

To prevent becoming a victim of the lack of adequate recruiting and selection process, firms should employ an organized strategy for talent acquisition. This involves defining clear job descriptions, completing extensive background checks, designing competency-based interview procedures, and applying assessment tools to analyze a candidate's skills, competencies, and cultural fit. The inclusion of numerous stakeholders, including HR experts, recruiting managers, and team members, may guarantee a fair and complete review process.

Furthermore, spending time and money in educating hiring managers on unconscious bias and adopting initiatives to promote diversity and inclusion may help decrease the risk of biased decision-making.

Implementing a good recruiting and selection procedure not only lowers risks but also enhances the possibility of finding the appropriate employees to contribute to the company's success. It guarantees that competent individuals are picked based on merit, boosting the possibilities of recruiting top talent and establishing a good and productive work environment.

In conclusion, the absence of an effective recruiting and selection procedure may be a huge business killer. It not only raises the risks of making erroneous hiring, but it also leads to a mismatch between credentials and job needs, encourages biased decision-making, and exposes firms to legal issues. To prevent these risks, firms must build comprehensive and disciplined recruiting and selection procedures that stress talent, diversity, and cultural fit. By doing so, organizations may improve their personnel, boost productivity, and position themselves for sustained development and success.

INSUFFICIENT TRAINING AND DEVELOPMENT PROGRAMS

Insufficient training and development programs may be a company killer. In today's fast-paced and competitive industry, organizations must invest in their workers' growth and skill development to remain ahead of the game. Failing to do so may result in a variety of negative repercussions that can significantly impair corporate performance.

One of the most visible repercussions of inadequate training and development programs is a deterioration in employee performance. When workers lack the essential training and resources to do their tasks successfully, their productivity and efficiency might suffer. This may lead to expensive errors, lost chances, and generally poor quality of work, eventually harming the company's bottom line.

Moreover, insufficient training may also contribute to a lack of desire and engagement among staff. When employees feel neglected and ill-prepared for their tasks, they may become disengaged, demotivated, and even unhappy. Without effective training programs that give continual growth opportunities, workers may feel stagnate in their jobs and seek chances elsewhere, leading to high turnover rates and a loss of talent.

Insufficient training and development programs may also limit innovation and advancement inside a corporation. As industries and technology advance, personnel need to continuously refresh their skills and expertise to stay up with the changing trends. Without access to professional development programs, workers may struggle to adapt to new technology and industry best practices, restricting the company's capacity to innovate and stay competitive.

Additionally, when workers feel undertrained and underappreciated, it may have a detrimental influence on the entire workplace culture and morale. A company that neglects training and development sends a message to its workers that their growth and development are not a priority. This may generate a feeling of discontent and irritation, leading to lower employee engagement, cooperation, and collaboration.

On the other hand, organizations that invest in thorough training and development programs may gain several rewards. For instance, well-trained personnel are more likely to be motivated, engaged, and confident in their responsibilities. They feel able to face difficulties and take on additional tasks, leading to greater productivity and work satisfaction.

Furthermore, a commitment to training and development helps recruit and retain outstanding people. Job candidates are increasingly seeking firms that provide prospects for growth and professional development. By offering effective training programs, firms may not only recruit highly skilled personnel but also retain them for the long term.

Investing in training and development also increases the company's image as an employer of choice. Organizations that emphasize the growth and development of their people are considered progressive and forward-thinking. This favorable image may recruit high-caliber applicants and establish a positive brand impression among consumers and clients.

To prevent the business killer of inadequate training and development programs, firms can take proactive efforts. Firstly, they should undertake detailed evaluations of staff abilities and identify areas where training is required. This might include technical skills, industry-specific knowledge, leadership development, and soft skills like communication and problem-solving.

Based on the evaluation, firms should plan and execute comprehensive training programs that address the identified shortcomings. These programs may involve a mix of in-house training, external workshops, seminars, online courses, mentoring, and coaching. It is vital to give continual training opportunities to ensure workers' abilities are up to date in a constantly changing corporate market.

Allocating regular resources and cash to training and development activities is crucial. This reflects the organization's commitment to employee advancement and highlights the need for ongoing learning. Companies can also build a supportive culture that promotes and compensates workers for taking advantage of training opportunities.

Additionally, it is vital to routinely examine the efficiency of training programs to ensure they are fulfilling the desired objectives. Gathering input from workers, measuring performance gains, and analyzing the influence on business objectives may assist modify and enhance training activities.

In conclusion, inadequate training and development programs may be damaging to a business's growth. By investing in comprehensive and continuous training efforts, firms can create competent and motivated workers, stimulate innovation, improve workplace culture, attract top talent, and ultimately avoid the business killer of insufficient training and development.

INEFFECTIVE PERFORMANCE MANAGEMENT AND FEEDBACK

Ineffective performance management and feedback may be damaging to any firm, functioning as a potential business killer. When managers do not adequately monitor and assess employee performance, it may lead to a loss in productivity, bad morale among workers, and ultimately, a decline in overall corporate success.

One significant reason why inadequate performance management and feedback may be negative is the absence of defined objectives and goals. When workers do not have a clear knowledge of what is expected of them, they may struggle to fulfill their objectives, resulting in mediocre performance. This lack of clarity may also produce uncertainty and irritation among workers, resulting in lower motivation and engagement with their job.

Another key problem with inadequate performance management is the lack of timely and constructive feedback. Regular feedback is vital for workers to understand how their performance corresponds with objectives and opportunities for growth. Without sufficient feedback, workers may continue to make the same errors or repeat unproductive behavior, impeding their development and success. This failure to course-correct may damage the overall success of the firm.

Additionally, inadequate performance management and feedback may contribute to an undesirable work atmosphere. When workers do not feel heard or respected, they might become disengaged and unsatisfied with their job. This may result in high turnover rates, higher absenteeism, and diminished overall team cooperation. The bad climate generated by inefficient performance management may extend across the firm, hurting not only individual workers but the whole team.

Moreover, inefficient performance management and feedback might impair professional development and career progression. Without frequent feedback and a clear awareness of their strengths and shortcomings, workers may struggle to discover areas for growth or potential for promotion. This lack of direction and support may lead to stagnation, preventing people from attaining their full potential and severely hurting their motivation and job satisfaction.

To prevent the potential business killer that inadequate performance management and feedback may pose, firms should prioritize establishing effective performance management practices. This involves establishing clear objectives and expectations, giving frequent and timely feedback, and delivering support and tools for staff growth. By investing in successful performance management, organizations can build a culture of responsibility, engagement, and continuous improvement, eventually driving success and avoiding the problems associated with inefficient performance management and feedback.

IGNORING EMPLOYEE ENGAGEMENT AND SATISFACTION

Ignoring employee engagement and happiness may be bad for any organization, as it can lead to lower productivity, high turnover rates, and a hostile work atmosphere. Failing to prioritize the well-being and engagement of workers is like playing with fire and may eventually grow into a business killer.

Engaged and pleased workers are the driving force behind a successful firm. They are enthusiastic, driven, and devoted to their job, resulting in increased production levels. When workers are engaged, they are more inclined to go the additional mile, take initiative, and provide unique ideas to the organization. On the other side, disengaged personnel might get complacent and may not put in the effort necessary to achieve in their professions.

Furthermore, disregarding employee engagement and happiness might lead to a high turnover rate. Dissatisfied workers are more inclined to seek employment elsewhere, resulting in a steady loss of talent for the firm. Hiring and training new personnel to replace those who leave may be expensive and time-consuming.

Moreover, the loss of experienced staff may significantly affect the overall performance and stability of the organization.

A lack of employee involvement and happiness may also produce a toxic work environment.

When workers feel devalued, unheard, or underappreciated, it may generate emotions of resentment and unhappiness.

A toxic work environment may lead to increased disagreements among workers, damaged relationships, and ultimately, a drop in morale and collaboration. The unpleasant environment may spread like wildfire, hurting not just the personnel directly engaged but also others around them.

Ignoring employee engagement and happiness may be a business killer since it affects the company's ability to recruit and retain outstanding personnel. In today's competitive employment market, workers have a broad variety of alternatives when it comes to selecting where to work.

A corporation that neglects employee engagement and happiness is unlikely to be recognized as an appealing employer. This might restrict the pool of eligible applicants who are willing to join the organization, making it harder to identify the appropriate personnel with the essential skills and fit for the company's culture.

To avoid falling into the trap of disregarding employee engagement and pleasure, firms should emphasize building a good work environment. This might entail developing employee appreciation programs, giving chances for growth and development, promoting open communication lines, and actively soliciting employee feedback. Regularly evaluating employee happiness via surveys and engagement evaluations may also assist in identifying areas of improvement and ensuring that the firm stays proactive in resolving any issues.

In conclusion, disregarding employee engagement and satisfaction may have major ramifications for any firm. Ignoring the well-being and motivation of workers may lead to lower productivity, high turnover rates, a hostile work environment, and difficulty in recruiting and maintaining top talent. To avoid becoming a business killer, firms need to encourage employee engagement and happiness, providing a good and happy work environment that supports productivity, loyalty, and success.

CHAPTER 10: CONCLUSION AND ACTION STEPS

Conclusion:

Avoiding business killers is vital for the success and survival of any firm. In this post, we have examined several frequent business killers and the solutions to combat them. Averting these possible problems demands a proactive approach and a deep awareness of the business environment.

Action Steps:

1. Identify the possible business killers: The first step towards avoiding business killers is to identify the elements that might significantly harm the firm. This involves studying the market, rivals, internal procedures, and client expectations. Conducting a comprehensive SWOT analysis and maintaining information about industry changes is vital.

2. build contingency plans: Once the possible business killers are identified, it is necessary to build contingency measures to limit their effect. These plans should detail the procedures to be followed in case of an unanticipated occurrence or a significant

market change. This will aid in reducing interruptions and preserving company continuity.

3. Improve risk management practices: Effective risk management is vital to prevent business killers. This entails identifying and managing risks connected with different corporate areas such as finance, operations, marketing, and human resources. Implementing effective risk management procedures will help the organization spot possible hazards in advance and take relevant steps.

4. establish a strong team: A competent and motivated team is vital for overcoming business killers. Investing in recruiting, training, and employee development programs may help establish a team that is capable of detecting and resolving potential business killers. Additionally, building a culture of cooperation, communication, and innovation inside the firm is crucial to promote proactive problem-solving and adaptation.

5. Stay knowledgeable and adaptable: The business world is always shifting, and new obstacles may appear unexpectedly. To prevent business killers, it is necessary to be educated about the newest market

trends, technology breakthroughs, and changing client needs. Regularly analyzing and reassessing the company plan and making required improvements will guarantee that the firm remains relevant and competitive.

6. Seek professional advice: It may be advantageous to seek the knowledge of experts or consultants who specialize in areas such as finance, marketing, legal compliance, and company strategy. Their excellent insights and recommendations may assist detect potential business killers and give suggestions on effective preventative actions.

7. Continuously monitor and assess performance: Regularly monitoring the firm's performance and key indicators is vital to spot any early symptoms of possible business killers. Implementing performance monitoring tools and performing frequent reviews will allow rapid response in case of any deviations from the planned results.

In conclusion, avoiding business killers needs a proactive strategy, solid risk management methods, and continual adaptability. By adopting these action actions, organizations may reduce the risks and navigate through the hurdles that might limit their performance. It is vital to remember that avoiding business killers is a continual process that involves awareness, agility, and a strong commitment to quality. By following these methods and keeping proactive, organizations may position themselves for long-term success and development.

www.ingramcontent.com/pod-product-compliance
Lightning Source LLC
Chambersburg PA
CBHW072200290526
45794CB00004B/1584